The
Haitian
Americans

CUBA

Windward
Passage

Île de la Tortue

North Atlantic
Ocean

Port-de-Paix

Cap-Haïtien

Gonaïves

Golfe de la Gonâve

Saint-Marc

Hinche

Île de la Gonâve

Hispaniola

Jérémie

PORT-AU-PRINCE

Miragoâne

Les Cayes

Jacmel

DOMINICAN
REPUBLIC

Caribbean Sea

| 0 | 30 | 60 km |
| 0 | 30 | 60 mi |

Haiti.

The Haitian Americans

Flore Zéphir

THE NEW AMERICANS

Ronald H. Bayor, Series Editor

GREENWOOD PRESS

Westport, Connecticut • London

Library of Congress Cataloging-in-Publication Data

Zéphir, Flore, 1958–
   The Haitian Americans / Flore Zéphir.
      p.   cm.—(The New Americans, ISSN 1092–6364)
   Includes bibliographical references and index.
   ISBN 0-313-32296-1
   1. Haitian Americans. I. Title. II. New Americans (Westport, Conn.)
E184.H27Z458   2004
973′.0049697294—dc22   2004011229

British Library Cataloguing in Publication Data is available.

Library of Congress Catalog Card Number: 2004011229
ISBN: 0–313–32296–1
ISSN: 1092–6364

First published in 2004

Greenwood Press, 88 Post Road West, Westport, CT 06881
An imprint of Greenwood Publishing Group, Inc.
www.greenwood.com

Printed in the United States of America

The paper used in this book complies with the
Permanent Paper Standard issued by the National
Information Standards Organization (Z39.48–1984).

10 9 8 7 6 5 4 3 2 1

Copyright Acknowledgments

The author and publisher gratefully acknowledge permission for use of the following:

Excerpts from Marguerite Laurent's poem "An Open Letter to the Little Girl in the Yellow Sunday
Dress" used by permission of Marguerite Laurent.

Contents

Series Foreword

Oscar Handlin, a prominent historian, once wrote, "I thought to write a history of the immigrants in America. Then I discovered that the immigrants were American history." The United States has always been a nation of nations where people from every region of the world have come to begin a new life. Other countries such as Canada, Argentina, and Australia also have had substantial immigration, but the United States is still unique in the diversity of nationalities and the great numbers of migrating people who have come to its shores.

Who are these immigrants? Why did they decide to come? How well have they adjusted to this new land? What has been the reaction to them? These are some of the questions the books in this "New Americans" series seek to answer. There have been many studies about earlier waves of immigrants—e.g., the English, Irish, Germans, Jews, Italians, and Poles—but relatively little has been written about the newer groups—those arriving in the last thirty years, since the passage of a new immigration law in 1965. This series is designed to correct that situation and to introduce these groups to the rest of America.

Each book in this series discusses one of these groups, and each is written by an expert on those immigrants. The volumes cover the new migration from primarily Asia, Latin America, and the Caribbean, including the Koreans, Cambodians, Filipinos, Vietnamese, South Asians such as Indians and Pakistanis, Chinese from both China and Taiwan, Haitians, Jamaicans, Cubans, Dominicans, Mexicans, Puerto Ricans (even though they are already U.S. citizens), and Jews from the former Soviet Union. Although some of these people, such as Jews, have been in America since colonial times, this series concentrates on their recent migrations, and thereby offers its unique contribution.

These volumes are designed for high school and general readers who want to learn more about their new neighbors. Each author has provided information about the land of origin, its history and culture, the reasons for migrating, and the ethnic culture as it began to adjust to American life. Readers will find fascinating details on religion, politics, foods, festivals, gender roles, employment trends, and general community life. They will learn how Vietnamese immigrants differ from Cuban immigrants and, yet, how they are also alike in many ways. Each book is arranged to offer an in-depth look at the particular immigrant group but also to enable readers to compare one group with the other. The volumes also contain brief biographical profiles of notable individuals, tables noting each group's immigration, and a short bibliography of readily available books and articles for further reading. Most contain a glossary of foreign words and phrases.

Students and others who read these volumes will secure a better understanding of the age-old questions of "who is an American" and "how does the assimilation process work?" Similar to their nineteenth- and early-twentieth-century forebears, many Americans today doubt the value of immigration and fear the influx of individuals who look and sound different from those who had come earlier. If comparable books had been written one hundred years ago they would have done much to help dispel readers' unwarranted fears of the newcomers. Nobody today would question, for example, the role of those of Irish or Italian ancestry as Americans; yet, this was a serious issue in our history and a source of great conflict. It is time to look at our recent arrivals, to understand their history and culture, their skills, their place in the United States, and their hopes and dreams as Americans.

The United States is a vastly different country than it was at the beginning of the twentieth century. The economy has shifted away from industrial jobs; the civil rights movement has changed minority-majority relations and, along with the women's movement, brought more people into the economic mainstream. Yet one aspect of American life remains strikingly similar—we are still the world's main immigrant receiving nation and as in every period of American history, we are still a nation of immigrants. It is essential that we attempt to learn about and understand this long-term process of migration and assimilation.

Ronald H. Bayor
Georgia Institute of Technology

Preface

The topic of the Haitian diaspora in the United States has been a research concern of mine for quite some time. In 1996 and 2001 respectively, I published two books on the subject. Therefore, it was with a great deal of interest and enthusiasm that I accepted Greenwood Press's invitation to write a reference work on the Haitian Americans, as part of The New Americans series. The series' intention to reach a broader audience, composed of high school and undergraduate college students, as well as general readers, was also a strong factor in my decision to come on board. Indeed, familiarity with, or knowledge of, the new ethnic groups that constitute the American mosaic should be disseminated to *all,* not just to a limited number of so-called specialists. Rightly, this knowledge belongs to the general public as it is part of the American patrimony.

As a Haitian immigrant myself, who has been in this country for thirty years, I have had countless opportunities to be asked about Haiti. In many of these instances, I have been (and continue to be) struck by the fact that many people know little about this Caribbean nation. Questions such as Where is Haiti?, What language do they speak there?, Who was it colonized by?, How come Haiti is so poor?, Why do so many Haitians want to come here?, In the news, you always hear bad things about Haiti—what is going on?, Is Duvalier still in Haiti?, Who is the president of Haiti now?, Is he doing anything for his people?, or even those of a more personal nature, You do not look like the Haitians I see on TV, are there different "races" of Haitians?, Why did you decide to come to this country?, guided my drafting of the historical section (chapters 2 and 3). This work provided me with an opportunity to address these questions. I hope that the information provided, although abridged, will satisfactorily answer most of them.

Once readers become familiar with Haitian history, they will understand why Haitian migration to the United States is high. In addition, as they gain some familiarity with the great migration history of this country and the various immigration laws, they will be able to assess in an informed manner the impact of current policies on newer immigrant groups, such as the Haitians.

In this work, I endeavor to present general facts about Haitians and to be as informative as possible. *The Haitian Americans* attempts to draw a broad picture of this group that depicts both their premigratory and postmigratory experiences. It places some emphasis on the continuity between the land of origin and the land of resettlement. The interconnectedness between events at home and the sociopolitical reality of this country is highlighted. Additionally, readers will follow these immigrants in their new communities, located in Miami's Little Haiti, Brooklyn's (New York) Flatbush Avenue, Mattapan's (Boston) neighborhood, and Chicago's South Side. They will learn about their successes and failures and the multiple factors that shape the outcome of their immigrant experiences. In short, I wish that *The Haitian Americans* will help the general reading public discover more about contemporary American society through the story of one of its major ethnic groups, the Haitians.

Acknowledgments

The real authors of *The Haitian Americans* are unquestionably the hundreds of Haitian/Haitian American men and women who allowed me into their homes and places of employment to record their varied perspectives. Although space constraints prevent me from acknowledging them by name, I wholeheartedly thank every single one of them, and I want them to know that without their contributions, the Haitian American experience could not have been inscribed in the larger American odyssey. I am grateful to them for placing their trust in me and for letting me be their voice. This is their book.

A work of this scope requires a great deal of both financial and human resources. First, I must acknowledge the University of Missouri at Columbia (MU), where I have had the privilege of teaching for the past 16 years. An MU Research Board grant provided me with the funds necessary to carry out fieldwork in Miami, Boston, and Chicago. In addition, it provided me with teaching replacement costs for the fall of 2002. My department, Romance Languages and Literatures, has always come through for me. Indeed, my former chair and associate chair, Professors Mary Jo Muratore and Marvin Lewis, were as enthusiastic as I was when I received an invitation from Greenwood Press to write this book. They guaranteed me release time one way or another, believing in the importance of my work and my ability to carry it to fruition. May they both find here the expression of my sincere gratitude.

The newer set of data was collected in Miami, Boston, and Chicago, and various individuals who contributed to the success of my fieldwork deserve special recognition. For Miami, I must thank Simone Dejean, Raymonde Bruny, Viter Juste, Claude Charles, Jean-Robert Cadely and his wife Carline Paul, Marleine Bastien, Gepsie Metellus, Louis Herns and Louise Marcelin, Rudolph Moise (and in particular his administrative assistant Ava Lampkin, who facilitated access to him), Jean Gervais, Yves Colon, Florence Verne, and Paul and Ginette Cadet for the wealth of information they generously shared with me. For Boston, I want to recognize Alix Cantave, Marc Prou, Michel DeGraff, Renote Jean-François, Lunine Pierre-Jerome, Lionel Hogu, Charlot Lucien, Fabienne Doucet, James Colimon, Steve Desrosiers, and William Dorcena for facilitating access to the Bostonian Haitian community and the city of Boston, with which I had no familiarity. For Chicago, I could not have done it without the help of Harry Fouché, Luce Marthol and her family, Aliette Marcelin, Gary and Marie Lyne Méhu, Clausel Rosembert, Émile André, Serge Pierre-Louis, and Janine Raymond. In addition, I am grateful to all my informants, who unselfishly shared their time, their patience, their hospitality, and their stories with me. *The Haitian Americans* has truly been a collective project.

Furthermore, I want to acknowledge Garry Pierre-Pierre and Bill Forry, publishers of the *Haitian Times* and of the *Boston Haitian Reporter,* respectively, for granting me permission to use several photographs published in their papers. In addition, I am grateful to Marguerite Laurent for allowing me to use exerpts from her poem in chapter 7. I also wish to convey my gratitude to Pierre Descieux, Jr., and Betty Jean-Baptiste for letting me use their pictures on the cover. They are our first introduction to the Haitian American community. Moreover, I want to express my thanks to all the individuals featured in the Appendix: Noted Haitian Americans, for putting up with my constant "harassment" in the form of numerous e-mails and phone calls. I am grateful for the information they provided and allowed me to print. Indeed, their stories of success burst with telling.

Additionally, I acknowledge my acquisition editor at Greenwood Press, Wendi Schnaufer, and Ronald Bayor from Georgia Institute of Technology, the series editor, for their careful examination of the manuscript and for helping me balance the rigors of academic scholarship with the interest of the general reader. The task was not easy, and at times conflicts arose. But in the end, the common desire to tell the Haitian American experience prevailed. I am grateful for their invitation and for their decision to publish my work on the Haitian diaspora. I am also indebted to Marry Harris for her willingness to lend me time and time again her sharp editing skills and unsurpassed knowledge of English grammar. Indeed, she read every single word of the manuscript and corrected my numerous stylistic infelicities.

And at last, always in a category of her own, my thanks go to my daughter Bambi, "my flesh thing," as I have many times referred to her. May the story of your people inscribed in these pages inspire you to "shoot for the moon" (to quote Kevin Lewis, a young African American friend)! And if you were to miss, that is okay too; you will still be "among the stars."

1

Introduction

HAITIAN IMMIGRANTS: THEIR LAND OF ORIGIN

Haitian immigrants in the United States come from the Caribbean island of Haiti, which is the original name given to it by its first inhabitants, the Tainos—a subgroup of the Amerindian people called Arawaks. It is believed that these Indians migrated north to this region some 2,000 years earlier from South America.[1] The Tainos called their island *Quisqueya* or *Bohio,* names that mean "vast country," or *Hayiti,* which means "mountainous land." It was the name *Haiti* that the former Black slaves decided to keep in 1804, when independence was won, making it the first Black republic of the world.

On December 5, 1492, aboard the *Santa Maria,* Christopher Columbus sighted the northern tip of a "very great island." He thought that this place was "the most beautiful in the world...almost like the lands of Castile; rather these are better."[2] For this reason, he called this island *Isla Española,* a name that later came to be pronounced *Hispaniola.* Present-day Haiti occupies the western third of the island of Hispaniola. In the north, it is bounded by the Atlantic Ocean; in the south by the Caribbean Sea; in the east by the Dominican Republic; and in the west by the Windward Passage, which separates it from the island of Cuba. The country's area is about 27,750 square kilometers, an area that is slightly smaller than the state of Maryland. The Dominican Republic comprises 48,730 square kilometers of the island. A couple of other small islands are also part of the Republic of Haiti. These include the island of La Gonâve, the biggest, located in the west, and the island of La Tortue, in the north, which is of historical significance as the spot where the first French settlers established themselves around 1640 to prey on passing Spanish galleon traffic crossing the Caribbean channel on their way to Sevilla with their treasures. The entire island of Hispaniola is part of the Greater Antilles. It is the second largest island of this group after Cuba, which has an area of 110,860 square kilometers; it is followed by Jamaica with an area of 10,990 square kilometers, and Puerto Rico with 8,900 square kilometers.

DEMOGRAPHY

The population of Haiti in 2002, according to the CIA World Factbook, was 7,063,722 inhabitants.[3] However, the Haitian Institute of Statistics and Data Processing (Institut Haïtien de Statistique et d'Informatique) places that number at 8,304,062.[4] With a current population growth of approximately 2 percent per year, this number could go up to 10 million by the year 2010.[5] The population of Haiti is ethnically very homogeneous, consisting of at least 95 percent Blacks; the remaining 5 percent is made up of Mulattoes, Syrians and Lebanese, and individuals of European descent (mostly Polish).[6] Most of the population reside in rural areas, where more than 5 million people live; only 3 million people are city dwellers. The major cities include Port-au-Prince, the capital, with close to 2 million people; Cap-Haïtien in the north, outside of which the famous Citadelle La Ferrière is located, with approximately 300,000 people; Les Cayes in the southwest, with a population of 250,000; and the historic city of Gonaïves—the cradle of independence, since it is where the former slaves proclaimed their independence from the French on January 1, 1804—with a population of about 200,000. Other sizeable cities include Jacmel and Jérémie in the south; Port-de-Paix in the north; and St. Marc in the center. Generally speaking, the population falls within the following age structure: 39.6 percent is under 15 years; 56.6 percent is between 15 and 64 years; and 3.8 percent is over 65 years.[7] The life expectancy of Haitians is 49.55 years, 51.29 years for females and 47.88 for males.

The two official languages of the country, according to the constitution of 1987, are French and Haitian Creole, the latter being referred to simply as *Creole* by the Haitians themselves. Creole is a language that developed in the seventeenth century on the plantations in the context of the French colonization of Saint-Domingue, as Haiti was named before its independence in 1804. Most of its vocabulary derives from French, and its syntax is based on the West African languages brought by the slaves, in particular a language called Ewe spoken in Ghana, Togo, and Benin. While the entire population speaks Creole, a much smaller segment—ranging from 5 to 20 percent of the population, depending on which estimates one relies on—speaks French. Generally speaking, French is spoken (in addition to Creole) in the urban centers by the educated sector; Creole is the sole means of communication of the masses living in rural areas and in the countryside. Haiti is predominantly a Catholic country, where 80 to 85 percent of the population practices this religion inherited from the French colonizers. Sixteen percent of the population is Protestant (10% Baptist, 4% Pentecostal, and 1% Adventist). However, in addition to being Catholic or Protestant, a significant portion of the population are Vodou believers and practitioners. Vodou (also spelled Voodoo, Vaudou, Vodu, or Vodun) is a religion that Haitians inherited from the African slaves who were brought to the French colony of Saint-Domingue. It is a mixture of West African religious traditions, consisting of a series of rituals (some involving animal sacrifices), dances, rhythms, and invocations to a variety of deities and spiritual beings (known as *lwas*).[8] One of the major aspect of this religion is its healing function. As one scholar explains,

> Vodou in Haiti is a religion that, through a complex system of myths and rituals, relates the life of the devotee to the deities who govern that life. Like many religions of the world, Vodou is a system of beliefs and practices that gives meaning to life: it uplifts the spirits of the downtrodden who experience life's misfortunes, instills in its devotees a need for solace and self-examination, and relates the profane world of humans to that of incommensurable mythological divine entities, called *lwas,* who govern the cosmos.[9]

Another scholar describes Vodou as more than a religious system: "throughout the whole of their nation's difficult history, the majority of Haitians have been agriculturalists, and as in other agricultural societies, philosophy, cosmology, medicine, religion, and justice systems are rolled into one worldview."[10] In the words of another authoritative anthropologist,

> Vodou offers doctrine, social controls, a pattern of family relations, direct communication with original forces, emotional release, dance, music, theatre, legend and folklore, motivation, alternative to threatening dangers, individual initiatives, through placation and invocation, treatment of ailments by means of herb lotions and rituals, protection of fields, fertility, and a continuing familiar relationship with the ancestors.[11]

The word *vodou* is said to be derived from two words in the language of the Fon tribe of Dahomey (present-day Benin): *vo,* which means "introspection," and *du,* which means "into the unknown." Conservative estimates place the number of Vodou adherents at 50 percent, but in reality this percentage is much higher. In fact, there is a popular saying that claims that 100 percent of the Haitian people serve the Vodou spirits.[12] The presence of Vodou is also well reflected in Haitian art; perhaps the most famous Haitian painter to rely on Vodou for his artistic creation is Hector Hyppolite.[13]

ECONOMY

Haiti is often referred to as the poorest country of the Western Hemisphere. Since its independence in 1804, the country has been plagued by endless political violence, which has been detrimental to the economic development of the country.[14] Haiti is mostly an agricultural country; the majority of the labor force (66%) is in the agricultural sector, 25 percent is in the service sector, and 9 percent is in the industrial sector. The average annual income by inhabitant is estimated at one hundred to two hundred fifty dollars. Moreover, there is widespread unemployment and underemployment since, according to the 2002 CIA World Factbook, more than two-thirds of the labor force do not have formal jobs. It is estimated that about 80 percent of the population lives below poverty level and that 70 percent depends on the agricultural sector. With regard to agriculture, the amount of arable land is very small, only 20 percent. This is caused to a large extent by the severe problem of deforestation that plagues Haiti. As one scholar observes,

> when Haiti was sighted by Columbus, it was more than 90 percent forested. Today only 2 percent of Haiti is forested, as trees have been cut down for firewood since 70 percent of Haiti's energy needs are met by charcoal (which is created from wood). The supply of arable land decreases by 3 percent annually. Deforestation and soil erosion are the major hindrances to rural development in Haiti.[15]

Haiti produces coffee, sugar, cocoa, and oils that are also used for export primarily to the United States. Most of the other crops produced are for local consumption, such as rice, corn, and millet. Although cash crops are produced by the peasants, their sale is outside of their control: it is regulated by the elite and the government. The fees and taxes levied for the export of coffee have placed a heavy burden on an already impoverished peasant class struggling to find arable land. As the supply of cultivable areas diminishes due to deforestation and overpopulation, the parcels of land that are cultivated are barely viable. In consequence, this situation has created a massive exodus of peasants from the rural areas to the towns, in search of scarce service or industry jobs. For example, one scholar reports that the population of Port-au-Prince, "estimated at about 500,000 in the 1970s, grew to well over a million by the end of the 1980s."[16] In the cities and towns, these migrant peasants find themselves living again on the margins, in slums. Some of the better-known slums in Port-au-Prince include Cité Carton (Cardboard City)—named after sheets of plastic or cardboard used to create separate rooms in shacks, themselves made of cardboard material—and Cité Soleil, which "houses about 400,000 people crammed without any of the basic amenities like water, electricity, or sanitation."[17] Tired of intermittent employment as unskilled laborers, or of being unemployed street people, many of them eventually consider going overseas *(à l'étranger);* their preferred destination is the United States. Shortly after, they become the boat people.

Moreover, Haiti imports heavily from foreign countries, among them the United States, Japan, and European countries. Food, manufactured goods, fuel, raw materials, machinery, and transport equipment comprise the majority of import commodities. The principal industries include sugar refining, flour milling, textile manufacturing, cement, and light assembly factories. These are owned by a small elite consisting mainly of Mulattoes, who control all of the export system with the collaboration of government officials who seek to gain from duties from export as well. According to the 2002 CIA World Factbook, Haiti has an external debt of over 1 billion dollars and is the recipient of 740 million dollars in economic aid. Its total expenditures exceed its revenues, leaving the country in a permanent budget deficit. Over the years, there have been a number of compelling external reports done by international agencies stating that foreign aid, instead of benefiting the people, has been siphoned off by high-ranking government officials, particularly under the Duvalier (Papa Doc and Baby Doc) administrations. It is also well documented that Jean-Claude Duvalier (Baby Doc) depleted the public treasury to satisfy his craving for yachts, luxurious villas, and expensive foreign cars, which he generously shared with his friends and mistresses.

Although the complex political history of Haiti is treated separately in chapters 2 and 3, it can be mentioned here that Haitian heads of state, more preoccupied with their own greed, have paid little attention to the socioeconomic affairs of the country. On the contrary, they have "squeezed and sucked" the peasants by imposing on them inequitable trade practices and tax burdens, without providing them with any social assistance whatsoever. Further, many analysts have argued that "the United States government, in turn, has consistently developed policies toward Haiti that benefits American trade and political and military supremacy."[18] The U.S. policies, as will be discussed later in chapter 3, have entailed maintaining the supposed right government in power. In short, for a variety of internal and external reasons, Haiti is composed largely of a disenfranchised majority, struggling every day to survive. Their efforts to survive have taken many of them to the shores of the United States.

Finally, the following information about education and health illustrates the magnitude of the problem that Haitians face due to the ongoing government neglect and the constant political chaos that have characterized Haiti since its independence. According to the Haitian constitution, education falls under the purview of the government and it is free. However, the number of public schools is alarmingly low. Out of an estimated total of 686 secondary schools, only 33 are public; similarly, less than 30 percent of the primary schools are run by the state. Moreover, it is reported that the quality of education in the public schools leaves a great deal to be desired and falls short of that offered in the private schools. Inadequate (and unsafe) facilities and buildings, insufficient school material and equipment, and lack of qualified teachers are all reasons cited to explain the substandard quality of Haitian public education. In consequence, only families who can afford to pay tuition send their children to school. This fact, in part, explains the high rate of illiteracy; approximately 78 percent of the population cannot read and write. With regard to health care, a report put out by the World Bank in 1995 states that only 2 percent of the population has access to medical services. It is estimated that Haiti has 0.1 doctors per 1,000 individuals; 0.5 hospital beds per 1,000 patients; 1 nurse per 100,000 patients; and 1 dentist per 200,000 individuals.[19] This shortage is due in part to the fact that many professionals left (and are still leaving) Haiti and relocated in the United States, Canada, Europe, and Africa, to flee political harassment. Infant mortality is relatively high at 7.1 percent, and life expectancy, as previously noted, is about 50 years.

In short, the Haitian landscape, muddied by political chaos, tainted by bloodshed, and stricken by poverty and lack of education and health care, is quite favorable to external migration. Throughout Haitian history, the United States has continuously received the bulk of the Haitian immigrants. Today, they constitute a sizeable diasporic population and are part of the New Americans, who are changing the color and the fabric of this country and who are receiving scholarly attention.

THE CHANGING OF COLORS

In the larger context of U.S. immigration, the arrival of Haitian immigrants is considered a relatively recent phenomenon that occurred in the twentieth century, more specifically the second half. The greatest wave of Haitian immigration occurred between 1991 and 2000, as a total of 179,644 legally entered the country, according to the records of the U.S. Immigration and Naturalization Service (INS). Immigrant groups, like Haitians, who entered the country after 1965, when more liberal immigration laws were enacted, are considered the New Americans, or perhaps the Newer Americans. Unlike the older flows, the newest arrivals do not come predominantly from Europe, but from Asia, Latin America, and the Caribbean. As one scholar notes, "the more than 20 million immigrants who have entered during this period have mostly come from dramatically different places than they did during the previous era." Indeed, it is reported that European nations sent approximately 15 percent of the latest waves of immigrants, that Asian nations supplied about 34 percent, and that nearly half of the total influx came from Third World regions of the Western Hemisphere.[20] According to the records of the Immigration and Naturalization Service, during the period 1971–1980, the total number of all immigrants to the country was 4,493,314. Out of that number, 800,368 were from Europe; this number represents 17.8 percent of the total. For the same period, immigration from Asia amounted to 1,588,178 people, or 35.3 percent; immigration from Mexico amounted to 640,294, and an emerging but steady Haitian immigration to 56,335. The number of non-European groups continued to increase in subsequent decades. During 1981–1990, over 2.7 million Asian immigrants came to this country, and almost another 2.8 million between 1991 and 2000. Over 1.6 million Mexicans arrived in 1981–1990, and over 2.2 million in 1991–2000. For the decade 1981–1990, 138,379 Haitians migrated to the United States. The beginning of the next millennium is witnessing the same phenomenon, and is consolidating the immigration patterns begun in the last decades of the twentieth century. Indeed, in the year 2000, only 14,532 immigrants came from the United Kingdom compared to 41,861 from China, 39,072 from India, 40,587 from the Philippines, 171,748 from Mexico, and 22,004 from Haiti.[21] It is predicted that by the year 2056, most Americans will trace their descent to "Africa, Asia, the Hispanic World, the Pacific Islands, Arabia—almost anywhere but white Europe."[22]

These numbers convincingly attest to America's changing colors, and these newest groups have begun to constitute the object of academic scholarship. Within this new tradition of scholarship, Haitian American Studies deserves coverage. It is the objective of the present reference volume to provide the general reading public with basic information about Haitian Americans in the United States. Who are the Haitians? Where did they come from? What are the characteristics of their land of origin? Why did they decide to come to the United States? Where have they established their communities? How well have they adjusted to their land of resettlement? How well have they been integrated into the labor market? What is the cultural baggage they brought with them from their homeland? What has been the U.S. reaction to them? What have been their interactions with other groups? What impact have they had on American society at large? Have they achieved the American dream? These are some of the questions that *The Haitian Americans* endeavors to answer. Readers will come away with a better understanding of this particular ethnic community, which constitutes a very visible segment of the American mosaic. They will find details on class stratification, politics, gender roles, employment trends, family life, education, art, music, literature, religion, foods, and general community organization. In short, their overall knowledge of the New Americans will be broadened.

The book comprises seven chapters. Chapter 1, the introduction, outlines the goals of the work and the major questions that it addresses. It discusses the methods used for data collection and the various mechanisms employed to obtain an accurate description of the Haitian immigrant community. Additionally, it provides a succinct examination of general immigration patterns to the United States and reviews immigration laws for specific groups, in an attempt to understand the environment into which Haitians have migrated. The chapter ends with a presentation of general facts and figures about Haitian immigration to this country.

Chapter 2, "Haiti: Colonial Times," offers a discussion of the early beginnings of Haiti with the arrival of European settlers. Then it moves into a description of French colonization, which underscores the social and economic conditions that existed in Haiti under colonialism. It ends with the Saint-Domingue revolution of 1791, which led to the establishment of a free nation.

The first part of chapter 3, "Haiti: The Making of a Nation," describes the birth of the nation and the proclamation of independence in 1804. It underlines the socioeconomic legacy of the revolution and explains the many challenges that faced the new nation, particularly with regard to its lack of recognition by the world powers. Additionally, it covers the U.S. occupation of Haiti (1911–1934). The second part of the chapter focuses on the Duvalier era, and the climate of dictatorship that characterized his regime. It also covers the post-Duvalier period that brought Jean-Bertrand Aristide to the political scene. Moreover, in light of these historical facts, it examines the various political and economic factors that cause massive numbers of Haitians to leave the country and to immigrate to the United States. The chapter concludes with a discussion of the development of a very indigenous Haitian ideology, which is reflected particularly in art, religion, and literary tradition, in spite of the country's political and economic challenges.

Chapter 4, "Coming to the United States," looks at specific immigration patterns and highlights their correlation with significant periods of Haitian history. It describes the different waves of Haitians and looks at their settlement patterns. It examines the climate of the host society toward Haitians by reviewing several well-known cases involving Haitians with immigration laws and the court system. It discusses Haitian immigrant dreams and American realities, and focuses on problems that Haitians encounter in the U.S. system, particularly in the labor market and in the schools.

Chapter 5, "No Longer Invisible: Haitian Ethnic Communities," describes specific Haitian communities in New York, Miami, Boston, and Chicago, which are among the major cities where Haitian immigrants have settled. It looks at community organization, media, businesses, schools, ethnic associations and neighborhoods, and major events in the community (historical and cultural). The chapter offers a portrait of Haitian ethnic life.

Chapter 6, "Making It in America: Haitian Immigrants' Ethnic Options," examines the mechanisms of survival used by Haitian immigrants to make it in America. It describes how this particular group organizes itself as a separate ethnic group in order to combat American racism and discrimination, and it highlights the parameters of Haitian ethnic identity, both for first and second generations. Moreover, it looks at Haitians' interactions with other groups, namely African Americans.

Chapter 7, "Haitian Impact on American Society," discusses Haitian immigrants' social mobility and assesses their success. It explores their contributions to American life in a variety of domains: literature, music, politics, economy, medicine, and education, among others. Finally, the chapter offers brief biographical profiles of successful Haitian immigrants. Others are presented in the Appendix.

This work is perhaps the first reference to offer the general reading public a profile of the Haitian diaspora currently residing in the United States, while including under the same cover some general information about Haitian history as well, which is necessary to understand the perspectives that Haitian immigrants bring with them. As such, the work fills a gap in the general (as opposed to specialized) literature on more contemporary U.S. ethnic groups, by focusing on one of the most recent groups to have migrated to the United States. Because of the newness of this particular group, compared to those of

European ancestry, very little is known about its history and culture or its mechanisms of integration in U.S. society. *The Haitian Americans* seeks to offer new generations of students and other readers a balanced picture of the Haitian diaspora in the United States, in an attempt to contribute to the overall knowledge of immigrant America.

The data on which this reference work is based come from a variety of sources. Various government publications, particularly those of the Immigration and Naturalization Service, were consulted in order to obtain accurate statistics and settlement distribution in the United States. An examination of these records revealed that the states of Florida (in the South); New York, Massachusetts, New Jersey, and Pennsylvania (in the Northeast); and Illinois (in the Midwest) received the highest number of Haitian immigrants. In light of these facts, fieldwork was conducted in representative cities of these regions—Miami, New York, Boston, and Chicago—that collectively can represent the majority of Haitian immigrants currently residing in the United States. Well-known community leaders—including directors of centers, school personnel, doctors, journalists, activists, and lawyers—were interviewed, and organizations and centers that cater to the Haitian communities were visited. Through this particular kind of ethnographic fieldwork, the Haitian diasporic life in the United States could be better presented to readers. It is therefore the aim of the present work to describe the Haitian American experience, and to explore in detail issues of adjustment and adaptation and to offer an overall assessment of Haitian American mobility.

OLD HAITIAN AMERICANS

Haitians are undoubtedly part of the New Americans who are changing the colors of this country. Indeed, they have been migrating in massive numbers during the last four decades of the twentieth century and are still disembarking every day on the shores of America. Like the earlier immigrants from Europe, they came in search of a new life, filled with opportunities that their homeland could not offer them. Although this work focuses on the so-called new Haitian Americans, it is relevant to indicate at the outset that the Haitian presence in the United States is not really new. In 1779, France sent a West Indian (Saint-Domingue, Guadeloupe, Martinique, and the smaller French islands) expeditionary force to help American Continentals defend Georgia and the Carolinas against the British. The contingent from Saint-Domingue (present-day Haiti) included *Affranchis* (freedmen) known as *chasseurs volon-*

taires de couleur (voluntary colored soldiers).[23] It is well documented that about 750 *chasseurs volontaires de couleur* helped the United States win its independence from England, fighting alongside American patriots against the British in the Siege of Savannah, in Georgia, on October 9, 1779. Currently this historical event is being recognized. As reported in the *Miami Herald* (June 13, 2002), under the auspices of the Haitian American Historical Society headquartered in Miami, plans are underway between Savannah officials and Haitian American elected officials in Miami-Dade County to begin a groundbreaking effort to commemorate Haitians' involvement in the U.S. Revolutionary War. It has been agreed that a monument will be built in the Battlefield Park Heritage Center, currently under construction near the Savannah battle site. Savannah Mayor Floyd Adams, Jr., pledged a plot of parkland to the Haitian American Historical Society, which is funding the construction of the Haitian monument.[24] In fact, in early December 2003, the city of Savannah held a two-day dedication ceremony at the location where the monument is slated to be erected. Regarding this memorial, the same *Miami Herald* article quotes North Miami Haitian American Mayor Josaphat (Joe) Celestin as follows: "It [the monument] means recognition of our efforts, that we were here all along, that Haiti was part of the effort to liberate America and that they [Haitians] came as free men, not as slaves." The monument will include a statue of Henry Christophe, one of the heroes of the Haitian revolution and the first king of Haiti, who is said to have participated in the battle as a 14-year-old drummer boy. Behind Christophe will be statues of other soldiers who were also involved in the battle; six panels inscribed with the soldiers' names will be added to the memorial. Among these *chasseurs,* names like André Rigaud and Jean-Baptiste Chavannes are of great significance to Haitian history (as is discussed in chapter 2). At the time of this writing, the Haitian American Historical Society is in the process of choosing a sculptor to design the monument and of raising the necessary funds. The experience of the Saint-Domingan soldiers in Savannah gives further meaning to what renowned American writer Herman Melville wrote over one hundred fifty years ago, in 1849: "You cannot spill a drop of American blood, without spilling the blood of the whole world. We are not a narrow tribe."[25]

Also in the eighteenth century, a well-known Haitian, Jean-Baptiste Pointe DuSable, founded the city of Chicago. An entire article is devoted to the "Haitian Father of Chicago" in the May 2002 issue of the *Boston Haitian Reporter.* The article reports that "in 1779, a handsome dark-skinned man built a sturdy wooden home on the North Bank of the Chicago River. A muscular, educated trader and fur trapper, Jean-Baptiste DuSable born in St.

Domingue—Haiti—was the first settler to put down stakes in what would become the 'Windy City,' earning him the appellation of the 'Father of Chicago.' DuSable was the son of a Haitian slave." DuSable's birth is traced to the city of St. Marc, Haiti, around 1745. He was born a free man, the son of a French sea captain and a Haitian slave. When he was a young man, DuSable's father sent him to France for his education; subsequently he traveled with his father on his merchant ships. It is reported that DuSable was injured aboard a ship on a voyage to New Orleans. However, when he arrived there, the 20-year old DuSable discovered that the city had been taken over by the Spanish and that he was in danger of enslavement. A local chapter of the French Jesuits hid him until he was well enough to sneak out of New Orleans and head north up the Mississippi River. In the region that would later become Illinois, he came in contact with French fur trappers and land speculators. In the early 1770s, he settled in Peoria, Illinois, where he sold furs and bought large amounts of acres of land. Soon, he became a wealthy business-man; subsequently he headed north toward the Great Lakes and established his home and thriving trading post on the bank of the Chicago River.[26] Cur-rently in Chicago, a coalition—the DuSable Park Coalition—is established to work with the Chicago Park District on the development of a three-acre parkland to commemorate Pointe DuSable's contributions to Chicago. This coalition is composed of various organizations, among them the Association of Haitian Physicians Abroad/Chicago Chapter and the Midwest Association of Haitian Women. Indeed, the Haitian American community in Chicago is active in memorializing DuSable's life; the activities of this community will be discussed in greater detail later.

Pierre Toussaint, considered the first American Black saint, is also of Hai-tian origin. He was born in 1778 of Haitian slaves in Saint-Domingue and was owned by a well-educated French Catholic family, the Bérards, who brought him to New York with them when they fled the slave uprising in 1797. While living with the family as a domestic slave, Toussaint learned to read and write and also learned how to be a hairstylist. It is said that he devel-oped a devoted clientele among the city's social elite and was allowed to keep some of his earnings. Among his distinguished clientele were the wife of Alexander Hamilton and the daughters of General Philip Schuyler, who had defeated the British at Saratoga. After Mr. Bérard died, his widow offered to grant Toussaint his freedom, but Toussaint then refused and supported her until her death. Her husband had left her with nothing, and the family had lost its plantation in Haiti. Nevertheless, she freed him before she died in 1807. Upon Mrs. Bérard's death, Toussaint married a woman from Haiti, and since they had no children of their own, they took in orphans, refugees, and other unfortunate people. In fact, he cofounded with Elizabeth Seton one of the first orphanages in New York City and helped with fundraising for the city's first cathedral. He also contributed money for New York's first Catholic school for Blacks on Canal Street. He died at the age of 87, regarded a saint by many.[27] In 1989, Cardinal John O'Connor of New York began to shepherd efforts for his canonization. He ordered Toussaint's remains exhumed in 1990 and moved to the crypt beneath the high altar of St. Patrick's Cathedral. He is the first person, other than an archbishop, to be buried there. In 1996, the Vatican declared Toussaint "venerable." During his October 1995 visit to New York and speaking to the faithful at St. Patrick's Cathedral, Pope John Paul II had this to say about Toussaint:

> Beneath the high altar of this Cathedral, together with the former cardinals and archbishops of New York, there is buried the servant of God, Pierre Toussaint, a married man, a one-time slave from Haiti. What is so extraordinary about this man? He radiated a most serene and joyful faith, nourished daily by the Eucharist and visits to the Blessed Sacrament. In the face of constant, painful discrimination he understood, as few have understood, the meaning of the words, "Father, forgive them; they do not know what they are doing." No treasure is as uplifting and transforming as the light of faith.[28]

The recognition of Pierre Toussaint has caught the attention of the Haitian community, and the Haitian Catholic Center located in the heart of Miami's Little Haiti has been renamed the Pierre Toussaint Haitian Catholic Center.

The Bérard family is just one example of several French families who fled Saint-Domingue from the 1790s through 1810. It is estimated that approximately 30,000 to 40,000 White colonists went to the United States, where the majority settled in French-speaking Louisiana and other regions of the antebellum South—Charleston and Savannah—while others (like the Bérards) sought refuge in New York, Philadelphia, and Boston. Several of these fleeing families brought their Black slaves with them.[29] The refugees from Saint-Domingue also included a couple of thousand Black freedmen. For example, in 1797, it was estimated that 1,335 "free Negroes" arrived in New Orleans; another contingent of 2,060 came later in 1809 by way of Cuba, where they had first sought refuge during the peak years of the Saint-Domingue revolution.[30] Black Saint-Domingans heavily influenced the folk culture of New Orleans, and they produced the most vibrant Black subculture of the antebellum South. Indeed, the calinda and bamboula dances well-known in New Orleans are said to have been brought by freed Blacks from Saint-Domingue. Just as dance forms originating from Saint-Domingue made their way into southern culture, religion also left its indelible marks. It is well documented that the Vodou religion in New Orleans began to blossom around 1800 with Sanité Dédé, a free woman of color from Saint-Domingue. The Saint-Domingan Vodou priestess was replaced in 1820 by New Orleans native Marie Laveau, who became legendary.[31] Today, visitors can see Marie Laveau's tomb in the St. Louis Cemetery (in New Orleans). Marie Laveau's House of Vodou located on 714 Bourbon Street is also a very popular tourist attraction. Incidentally, some of the magical, vodouesque quality of Black Louisianans is well depicted in the contemporary movie *Eve's Bayou,* released in 1997.

Furthermore, people of color and Blacks from Saint-Domingue became very active in the abolitionist movement of the United States. In Philadelphia, for example, they formed their own political organization, known as Les Citoyens de Couleur de Philadelphie, and fought for the advancement of Black Americans. In fact, several Saint-Domingans became leaders in American communities and had an impact on agriculture and business. In Louisiana in 1795, a man of color from Saint-Domingue named Jean Etienne Boré revolutionized the sugar industry by designing new methods for manufacturing sugar. Relying on the technology used in the sugar production in Saint-Domingue, he converted cane juice into granules that could be stored and shipped easily. He was so successful and so well known in the community that in 1803 he became the first mayor of the city of New Orleans. It is also reported that James Pitot, a former refugee from Saint-Domingue, succeeded Boré as the city's second mayor, serving from June 2, 1804, to July 26, 1805. Other Saint-Domingans prospered in Savannah in the tailoring business and owned significant real estate. In the same connection, in Baltimore in 1829, four colored Saint-Domingan women—Elizabeth Lange, Marie Magdelene Baas, Marie Rose Boegue, and Marie Therese Duchemin—established the Oblate Sisters of Providence, the world's first Black religious community, and founded the School for Colored Girls. Students from the neighboring cities of Philadelphia and Washington, D.C., attended the Oblates' school. Subsequently, the Oblates became a national institution, with schools in St. Louis and Charleston educating Black children.[32]

Another important figure of Saint-Domingan origin is John James Audubon, who is considered one of the world's greatest ornithologists. According to the National Audubon Society, he was born on April 26, 1785, in the southern city of Les Cayes. He was the illegitimate son of a French naval lieutenant, Jean Audubon, and a Creole woman. When he was a young boy, his mother was killed in a slave uprising and he went to Nantes, where he was raised by his stepmother. Subsequently, he moved to Pennsylvania to oversee the family-owned estate at Mill Grove, near Philadelphia. It was on this farm that he developed his fascination for birds and set out to depict America's avifauna. His passion for ornithology is well reflected in his major illustrative works, *Birds of America* and *Viviparous Quadrupeds of North America*. John James Audubon's legacy as an avid naturalist and a keen observer of birds is unsurpassed. Indeed, the National Audubon Society continues to carry his name and his legacy throughout the United States.

All these facts that are now beginning to be known and brought to the reading public's attention convincingly attest that Haitians have long been making their impact on U.S. society. One of the objectives of this work is to document this impact and to accurately describe the Haitian American experience in a country that has always been a nation of immigrants.

THE NEW AMERICANS

One scholar describes America as a "multicultural event."[33] This metaphor is quite relevant when one looks at the history of immigration to this country, documenting the fact that people from all over the world came to the shores of America at various points in time, beginning in the early part of the sixteenth century. Indeed, the fabric of American society has always been a mosaic of cultures and nationalities. The nature of this mosaic has evolved significantly throughout the years, and in the nineteenth century profound shifts in the ethnic origins of immigrants began to occur. The term *new Americans* was first introduced refer to during the first half of the twentieth century to immigrants who entered the country in the second half of the nineteenth century. As a result of the changing character of U.S. immigration, many restrictive laws were enacted between the late 1880s and the mid-1930s, and they remained in effect until the 1960s with the Civil Rights Revolution.

"World War II was the transition to the Civil Rights Revolution," writes one scholar.[34] The yearning for democracy in Europe triggered demands for racial justice in the United States. In the 1960s, as the country entered the age of globalization, the forces of democracy and more liberal tendencies began to permeate the political institutions. The election of President John F. Kennedy facilitated the promulgation of more liberal immigration policies. Moreover, the Black Civil Rights movement was relentlessly pushing the United States to reevaluate its position on issues of race and ethnic minorities. The concerns of the period led to the Civil Rights Act of 1964 and to the Immigration Act of 1965. This piece of legislation reopened the so-called golden door and allowed the legal admission of hundreds of thousands of new immigrants per year, beyond quotas. The post-1965 flow of immigration was quite different from previous flows in the sense that the majority of immigrants came primarily from Asia, Mexico, Latin America, and the Caribbean. In addition to changes in the immigration laws that attracted massive numbers of people from these regions, strong push factors (adverse conditions in countries of origin), such as civil wars, economic pressures, and social and political instability, also accounted for this overwhelming migration. For example, the rise of Fidel Castro in Cuba in 1959 led to a massive migration of Cubans; communist victories in Asia triggered an enormous exodus of Southeast Asians. During the 1960s and 1970s, for example, 400,000 refugees arrived from Cuba; 340,000 from Vietnam, the majority coming to the United States after the fall of Saigon to the North Vietnamese; 110,000 from Laos; nearly 70,000 from Cambodia as a result of the Cambodian Civil War 1969–1975; and 34,499 from Haiti, many fleeing the dictatorship of François "Papa Doc" Duvalier from 1961–1970; in addition to other refugees from the Soviet Union, Rumania, Poland, and Czechoslovakia.[35] With the continuous flow of legal immigration also came illegal immigration. It is estimated that millions of immigrants have entered the country illegally since the 1960s, and in 1984 alone it is reported that the Immigration and Naturalization Service apprehended over 1.2 million undocumented immigrants.[36] The government saw a pressing need to control illegal immigration, and this led to the 1986 Immigration Reform and Control Act, known as the IRCA. Subsequently, in 1990 Congress rushed to enact new immigration reforms that set new ceilings for worldwide immigration. More recently, in 1996, the Illegal Immigration Reform and Immigrant Responsibility Act was passed as another attempt to reverse the continuous surge of illegal immigrants into the United States. In October 1996, the Immigration and Naturalization Service estimated the number of the total illegal population at 5 million, and it included Haiti as one of the top five countries of origin for illegal immigration, Mexico being the first.[37]

This succinct review of U.S. immigration history and policies enables us to understand that in a very real sense the United States is unquestionably a nation of immigrants, all of whom have come from somewhere else at different periods of time for basically the same reason: the search for prosperity and happiness. It is, therefore, in the context of American immigration that we will begin our description of the Haitian Americans.

THE NEW HAITIAN AMERICANS

As stated at the beginning of the chapter, the first Haitian presence in the United States dates back to the second half of the eighteenth century, when 750 soldiers from Saint-Domingue joined forces with American troops and participated in the Battle of Sanannah in 1779. Toward the end of the century, as Saint-Domingan slaves revolted to fight for their freedom against French colonialism, several of these Whites fearing for their lives fled to America and brought a small number of slaves with them. Haitian immigration to the United States remained very small until the second half of the twentieth century. During the U.S. occupation of Haiti (1915–1934), a relatively important group of Haitian immigrants migrated to the United States, ironically fleeing the atrocities of the occupation. There were approximately a couple hundred of them, and they came from urban areas of Haiti. It is reported that most were scattered throughout New York City and that they interacted with other Negro groups.[38] The Immigration and Naturalization Service began recording separately Haitian immigration in 1932; for the period 1932–1940, it recorded 191 Haitian immigrants, and it recorded 911 from 1941 to 1950. In the decade that followed (1951–1960), 4,442 more Haitians were recorded. However, since the 1960s, as a result of the 1965 Immigration Act, Haitian immigration to the United States increased drastically, as INS records document:

Period	Number of Immigrants
1961–1970	34,499
1971–1980	56,335
1981–1990	138,379
1991–2000	179,644

In short, from 1932 through 2000, a total of 414,401 Haitians immigrated legally to the United States.[39]

However, it is important to note that there is a substantial amount of illegal Haitian immigration that started in the early 1970s. Several Haitians attempting to escape the dictatorship of the Duvalier regime, which consolidated itself during the reign of Jean-Claude "Baby Doc" Duvalier—son of François Duvalier, also self-proclaimed president-for-life—simply overstayed their visas, in the hope of legalizing their status some day. Additionally, the growing political instability of the post-Duvalier years (1986 to present) continues to incite nonimmigrants admitted on temporary visas to stay in the United States. For example, in 1999 alone, there were 85,224 nonimmigrant

Haitians admitted to this country, in addition to already 874,095 between 1985 and 1996.[40] The category of nonimmigrants—temporary visitors for business and pleasure, students, transit aliens, temporary workers and trainees—provides the largest number of illegal aliens. It is estimated that half of the Haitians admitted as nonimmigrants do not return to Haiti; this brings the number of the total illegal population closer to 500,000, as opposed to the conservative estimate of 105,000 recorded by the Immigration and Naturalization Service in 1996.[41] Moreover, scores of other Haitians fleeing political persecutions decided to make their 700-mile sea journey to the South Florida coast in small, rickety boats. They became known as the *boat people,* and it is estimated that 40,000 Haitian boat people arrived as early as 1980–1981. To this day, Haitian boat people continue to disembark on the shores of South Florida. The *Haitian Times* (November 6–12, 2002, issue, p. 12) reports that for fiscal year 2001, the U.S. Coast Guard "interdicted" 1,391 Haitians, and they stopped another 1,486 at sea between October 2001 and September 2002. Moreover, on December 3, 2001, a boatload carrying 167 people was intercepted. This event received a great deal of media coverage on all the news networks. Most of these Haitians are held in the Krome Processing (Detention) Center and the women are kept in the Turner Guilford Knight Correctional Center in Miami, awaiting a review of their claims for asylum by the Immigration and Naturalization Service. More recently, on October 29, 2002, another load of 206 people made it to the Miami shores, as their boat ran aground. Video footage from all major news networks showed Haitians jumping in the water and running onto the Rickenbacker Causeway, which leads to Miami, stopping traffic. They were picked up by the Miami police and taken to the Krome Processing Center to await their fate from the Immigration and Naturalization Service. For 1999, Haiti ranked third in the number of new claims for asylum, with 2,492 cases filed; this number is in addition to the 14,823 cases pending at the beginning of the year and the other 548 cases that were reopened during the same year.[42] Moreover, between 1993 and 1999, 6,763 Haitian refugee arrivals were recorded.[43] Based on all these figures, it is not unreasonable to estimate the total number of Haitians (legal and illegal) in the United States at close to one million. This work will trace the courageous journey of these people from their homeland to their new world.

In the following chapter, a historical background that takes the reader from Haiti's colonial times through its birth as a free nation is offered. Then, the historical discussion continues in chapter 3 with the making of the Haitian nation from independence to contemporary times. Since the Haitian diasporic experience is firmly grounded in its history, it is critical to have some

Haitian boat people intercepted and "inspected" on October 29, 2002, by police officers wearing masks. Courtesy of the *Haitian Times.*

familiarity with this nation's past; it is against this historical backdrop that Haitian migration must be understood. In the words of the president of the greater-Miami American Civil Liberties Union, Lida Rodriguez-Taseff, "we need to look at the cause of why these people are coming and running away."[44] The cause of this massive Haitian migration resides precisely in the political history of the country.

NOTES

1. Arthur and Dash (1999: 17).

2. Heinl, Heinl, and Heinl (1995: 12).

3. The 2002 CIA World Factbook can be found at the following Web site: http://www.cia.gov/cia/publications/factbook/geos/ha.html#Intro.

4. The information provided by the Institut Haïtien de Statistique et d'Informatique is available through the New York Haitian Consulate's Web site: http://www.haitianconsulate-nyc.org/demographie.html.

5. Arthur (2002: 6).

6. Arthur (2002: 7–8) reports that some 2,570 Polish mercenaries were sent by Napoleon in 1803 in his attempt to suppress unsuccessfully the slave revolutionary movement. These Polish remained in Haiti after its independence; their descendents are part of the Haitian population. Arthur also goes on to say that another group of 15,000 people from the French Levantine territories of the Middle East arrived in the late nineteenth and early twentieth centuries, and they prospered as traders and merchants. Their descendants are among the prominent members of the business community.

7. Institut Haïtien de Statistique et d'Informatique, available through the New York Haitian Consulate's Web site: http://www.haitianconsulate-nyc.org/demographie.html.

8. For more on Vodou rituals, dances, and rhythms, see Fleurant (1996). Galembo (1998) is also a good reference book on Haitian Vodou, buttressed by beautiful photographs.

9. Desmangles (1992: 2–3).

10. McAlister (2002: 10–11).

11. Courlander (1960), as quoted in Arthur (2002: 75).

12. Brown (2001: 5).

13. A good reference for Haitian art is Alexis (2000). In addition, this work has wonderful photographs of Haitian paintings. More is said about Haitian art in chapter 3.

14. The political history of the country strongly explains Haitian immigration. As such it is treated separately in chapters 2 and 3.

15. Dash (2001: 2).

16. Ibid., p. 40.

17. Ibid., p. 41.

18. McAlister (2002: 11).

19. This information is found on the following Web site: www.haiticulture.ch/Haiti.html.

20. LeMay and Barkan (1999: xxxvii).

21. United States Department of Justice, Immigration and Naturalization Service, 2000 *Statistical Yearbook,* Table 2, p. 9.

22. Takaki (1993: 2).

23. For more on this, see Heinl, Heinl, and Heinl (1995: 34–35).

24. The Haitian American Historical Society is located at 8340 N.E. Second Avenue, Suite 222, Miami, FL 33138. The chairperson of the society, Daniel Fils-Aimé, can be reached at (786) 621-0035 or at hahs@haitianhistory.org.

25. Herman Melville's *Redburn,* as quoted in Takaki (1993: 427) and Takaki (1998: 5).

26. Most of the information about DuSable came from the May 2002 issue of the *Boston Haitian Reporter* (p. 25). Although information about his birth is somewhat murky, Walker (1999: 23) confirms that he was born in Santo Domingo. Chicago historian Quaife (1933: 36) asserts that he was "base born," and that "his mother was probably a slave." He further indicates that DuSable himself described himself as a "free negro."

27. The source of most of the information on Pierre Toussaint comes from a Web site put out by the Franciscan University of Steubenville, Ohio, in honor of Black History Month: www.bcimall.org/calendar/franuniv/pierre_toussaint.htm.

28. Various other Web sites provided additional information on Pierre Toussaint pertaining to the Vatican's recent recognition of his sainthood.

29. Brownstone and Franck (2001: 515).

30. Hunt (1988: 46–47).

31. Ibid., pp. 77–80.

32. Some of the information about the early Saint-Domingan/Haitian presence in the United States comes from Pamphile (2001: 8–16). Other information is based on various Web sites.

33. Takaki (1993: 427).

34. Ibid., p. 399.

35. LeMay and Barkan (1999: 272). The number for Haiti is taken from the Immigration and Naturalization Service, 2000 *Statistical Yearbook.*

36. LeMay and Barkan (1999: xxxvii).

37. Brownstone and Franck (2001: 749–52).

38. See Laguerre (1984: 23) and Reid (1939: 97–98).

39. Immigration and Naturalization Service, 2000 *Statistical Yearbook,* Table 2, pp. 8–9.

40. Immigration and Naturalization Service, 1999 *Statistical Yearbook,* Table 36, p. 135. See also Zéphir (2001: 7–10).

41. Immigration and Naturalization Service, 1999 *Statistical Yearbook,* p. 241.

42. Ibid., p. 86 and p. 102 (Table 27), respectively.

43. Ibid., Table 24, p. 95.

44. As quoted in a CNN report, "Detained Haitians Wait to Learn Fate," published on the Web on October 30, 2002, at http://www.cnn.com/2002/US/South/10/30/haitians.ashore/index.html.

2

Haiti: Colonial Times

Haitian immigrants came to the United States with a "baggage of things past." The baggage of the past includes their values, culture, aspirations, conceptions, and beliefs about who they are and where they are going as a people. All of these are shaped by a series of historical events that led to the creation of their country as an independent nation in 1804 and have had an impact on its development henceforth. History has undoubtedly molded the character of the Haitian people, landscape, and society. Three significant periods characterize this history: colonization, which began with the arrival of the Europeans; the slave revolution, which lasted 12 years and culminated in Haiti's independence; and the postindependence era, filled with political instability and unrest to the present day. Contradictions, conflicts, clashes of interests, social stratification, prejudice, and misery have marked all three periods. Ironically, the Haitians have always been searching for a better life: as slaves, they yearned for their freedom, fought and died for it; as free men, they aspired to become autonomous farmers and owners of the lands they cultivated; as Haitians, they longed to come out of poverty and experience the basic commodities of the modern world—employment, shelter, food, clothing, education, health care, and the pursuit of happiness, free of persecution. Now, as immigrants in the United States, they want to be treated with dignity and to enjoy the benefits of prosperity in a country where democracy flourishes and where hard work is rewarded.

In the course of their immigration experience, Haitians remain rooted in their past, that of the revolution and independence. They cherish their heroes—Boukman, Toussaint Louverture, Dessalines, Christophe, and

Pétion, among others—and admire their great thinkers and writers—Jacques Roumain, Jean Price-Mars, and Félix Morisseau-Leroy, for example. It is, therefore, not by accident that two major thoroughfares in Miami's Little Haiti—Second Avenue N.E. and 54th Street—have been renamed Avenue Morisseau-Leroy, after the revered Haitian poet who spent the later years of his life in Miami, and Toussaint Louverture Boulevard, respectively, and that an elementary school also in Little Haiti bears the name of Toussaint Louverture. Likewise, sections of Nostrand Avenue in Brooklyn, New York, from the intersection with Eastern Parkway to the junction with Flatbush Avenue, have also been renamed Toussaint Louverture Boulevard. In a similar connection, it is also not by accident that the Haitian-American United Association of Boston has instituted the Haitian Heritage Month along with the Annual May Haitian Unity Parade, and the Haitian Independence Gala as well, to commemorate the achievements of Haitians and Haitian Americans. Further, it is not by mere coincidence either that retired senator Bill Owens, in his remarks delivered on January 5, 2002, at the Haitian Independence Gala, stressed the impact of the Haitian Revolution in the United States:

> The Haitians proclaimed their independence on January 1st 1804, an event which stands as an eloquent testimony to the strengths and unity of the human spirit. The Haitian revolution belongs to the Haitian people, but above all, it belongs to all people struggling for freedom, peace, and justice. And to us, struggle for independence from England.[1]

In the same address, the distinguished American senator went on to acknowledge the Haitian involvement in the Battle of Savannah, Georgia. In the same vein, it is also not by coincidence that on May 22, 2003, the governor of the state of New York, George E. Pataki, issued a proclamation to honor the 200th anniversary of the Haitian Flag. In his address, Governor Pataki stated:

> **Whereas,** this occasion is furthermore significant in that it commemorates the events leading to the birth of the Haitian Flag on May 18, 1803 and the establishment of the first black republic in 1804; as the first *free* black republic, Haiti's unique role inspired people worldwide and represented the hopes of enslaved people throughout the globe to be free.[2]

In the following pages, a historical background is offered that traces the origins and causes of significant Haitian events, out of which many now-celebrated heroes were born, and events that have shaped the Haitian American character.

THE SPANISH CONQUEST OF HAYITI

The Spanish, led by Christopher Columbus, were the first Europeans to set foot on the northern tip of an island that Columbus named Hispaniola, on December 5, 1492. At the time of Spanish arrival, the island was inhabited by the Tainos, a subgroup of the Amerindian people called Arawaks (as can be recalled from chapter 1). The Spanish quickly noted that the Tainos decorated themselves with gold; they wanted that gold. In consequence, they ordered these gentle people to dig them the yellow metal and to cultivate new crops they had introduced, namely sugar. If the year 1492 marks the so-called discovery of Haiti, as many historians like to refer to this historical event, it undoubtedly marks the beginning of slavery in this part of the world. As a matter of fact, the Spaniards, immediately after their arrival, transformed the "very great island" of Hispaniola into an island of slaves; the lands of the Tainos, in the most absolute sense, became the lands of Castile. The Tainos were put to forced labor, their main chore being the extraction of gold from mines, rivers, and streams. Not used to this kind of regimen, the Taino population was decimated rapidly. Thousands of them died; scores of others committed suicide; others rebelled, escaped to the mountains, or fought the Spanish, but were later caught and killed. In addition, staggering numbers died of diseases, previously totally unknown in the Americas, that were introduced by the Europeans. Within a decade after their arrival, the Spanish were responsible for the extermination of most of the Taino population. Therefore, to replenish the labor supply, the Spanish, as early as 1500, brought African slaves to Hispaniola. Based on the report of an eighteenth-century chronicler, Père Charlevoix, it is believed that Christopher Columbus himself brought the first Blacks with him to the New World, when he returned to Hispaniola after a trip from Spain.[3] To halt the Indian hecatomb, Bishop Bartolomé de Las Casas pleaded with the king of Spain to bring Africans to the West Indies. The Spanish liked the idea, and soon after the slave trade from Africa began.

In the successive decade, Spanish colonial enterprise shifted more to eastern Hispaniola (the region that is the present-day Dominican Republic), which was richer in gold, and contingents of African slaves were brought to work the Cibao gold mines in the region where they founded the city of Santo Domingo. As it turned out, this eastern location was also a good base for the Spanish to explore South America, as the gold of Cibao was petering out. It is said that very little gold was produced after 1515 and that all mining virtually ceased by 1519.[4] The cultivation of crops was the only thing left to do in Hispaniola. Therefore, the greedy Spanish, not interested in agriculture but in new gold, began to leave Hispaniola and moved on to Panama,

Cuba, Puerto Rico, and later Mexico and Peru, which by mid-sixteenth century had been taken over by Spanish conquistadors. By the end of the sixteenth century, large amounts of land in the western part of Hispaniola had been deserted. These vacant lands became ideal locations for marauding bands of European mercenaries, among them French hunters and pirates who settled on Tortuga Island (so named by Columbus, and translated in French as l'île de La Tortue, the name used in present-day Haiti) located six miles off the northwestern tip of Hispaniola.

THE FRENCH CONQUEST OF HISPANIOLA

All throughout the sixteenth century, Spain's claimed sovereignty over the New World did not remain unchallenged. Other Europeans disagreed with Spanish rulers' assertion that the Caribbean islands were their property because Columbus had discovered them and established settlements there under the authority of the Spanish Crown (Queen Isabella). They envied the wealth the Spanish had amassed in the Caribbean. War broke out; soon, piracy became an accepted business, and hordes of pirates began attacking Spanish ports. Many even sailed the trade winds to the Caribbean, where they positioned themselves on vacant lands to prey on Spanish galleon traffic crossing the Caribbean channel on their way to Seville with their treasures. The French, who were continuously at war with Spain, are said to be the first to attack Spain's Caribbean ports. These attacks were orchestrated by naval squadrons belonging to French corsairs from the region of Normandy. It is believed that French pirates outnumbered those from other nations during most of the century. Many of these Norman pirates established themselves on Tortuga Island, a strategic base situated between two straits—the Windward Passage and the Mona Passage—well traveled by ships.[5] According to a prominent Haitian historian, once established on this small island, some of these pirates continued their fearsome plundering. They are known in the literature as the *freebooters* or *flibustiers* (in French). Aboard flimsy boats ("fly boats," from which their name is said to be derived), they harried the Caribbean commerce of Spain. However, another group of these original Tortugan pirates eventually tired of the perils of piracy. They began to settle down, making a living out of hunting the wild cattle and pigs that had multiplied on the island (originally brought by the Spaniards). This group of French hunters is referred to as the *buccaneers*. The term arose from their major activity: they cured and processed their meats on an open fire called *boucan*, a frenchified version of the Indian word *boucacoui*, which is a process for smoking meat. The buccaneers supplied the freebooters with food and sold them animal hides. The hunting and selling activities of the buccaneers took them across the short Tortuga channel, on the northern coast of the main island. Little by little, they settled, conquered the forest, cleared the land, and devoted themselves to agriculture.[6] These *habitants* were soon joined by a small group of other French, namely Protestants called Huguenots, who were fleeing religious discrimination from the Catholic French government and who harbored strong resentment against Catholic Spain as well. The western part of the island of Hispaniola was gradually being populated by French, and historians establish the French presence in western Hispaniola as early as 1640.

The looting activities in which the freebooters engaged made them feared by the Spanish (and other Europeans, namely the English and the Dutch, who also fought for the region during the same period) and gave them autonomy on this part of the island of which they became unquestionable landlords. It is also documented that these freebooters had slaves with them, most stolen from the Spanish in mainland Hispaniola and the Portuguese near the Orinoco basin. Moreover, the feats and prowess of the freebooters and buccaneers became known to the French Crown. Therefore, France, still at odds with Spain, thought it could use these citizens to firmly establish its own colony on this island and to take some of the profits from its rival. Consequently, it chartered the French West Indies Company (Compagnie des Indes Occidentales) in March 1664 to consolidate its trade and holdings in the West Indies, as well as those of individual French subjects, namely those same buccaneers and freebooters. Subsequently in 1665, Colbert, Louis XIV's first minister, chose to appoint a governor to the French part of Hispaniola, now renamed Saint-Domingue. Bertrand d'Ogeron's appointment as governor in 1665 marks the official establishment of the French colony of Saint-Domingue. The new colony immediately began to prosper, and the number of French settlers, apprised of fortunes to be made in the New World, increased considerably in subsequent years. The cultivation of tobacco and sugar was continued; new crops such as coffee, cocoa, cotton, and indigo were also introduced. Under d'Ogeron's administration, which lasted until 1674, more mainland cities were settled (Port-de-Paix, and Cap-Français—now Cap-Haitian—for example), and Saint-Domingue was well underway to becoming a profitable colony. While Saint-Domingue was emerging as a prosperous French colony in the New World, Europe itself was waging a nine-year war (1688–1697) that opposed Spain and France, among other nations. The war ended with the Treaty of Ryswick, according to which Spain, in September 1697, conceded the western third of the original island of Hispaniola to France.

THE FRENCH COLONY OF SAINT-DOMINGUE

The Treaty of Ryswick officially allowed France to begin its 100 years of colonization over western Hispaniola. Saint-Domingue was transformed into a lucrative agricultural society, where crops such as sugar, indigo, coffee, cotton, and cocoa were intensely cultivated. The cultivation of these crops required an immense labor force; consequently, the French rapidly perpetuated the slave trade from Africa that the Spanish had started almost two centuries earlier. The census of 1791 estimates the slave population at 500,000, but authoritative Haitian historian Thomas Madiou suggests that the actual slave population was closer to 700,000, since colonists deliberately underreported slave numbers for tax evasion purposes.[7] Saint-Domingue made up three-fifths of the entire slave population of all French colonies in the Americas. By the mid-eighteenth century, it had become the most prosperous of all colonies in the New World and was known as "the pearl of the Antilles." In 1791 on the eve of the slave revolution, Saint-Domingue's exports to France were equivalent to $41 million, and its net worth was put at $300 million.[8] A small group of large plantation owners and merchants known as the *grands blancs* accumulated huge fortunes. To acknowledge the wealth of these planters, the expression "rich as a Créole" (referring to French born or living in the colony as opposed to France) became common in France. However, in spite of its prosperity and productivity, Saint-Domingue, as some historians have noted, was "a very sick society at war with itself" and fraught with internal inconsistencies and contradictions.[9] Its fragile success was based on French capital and slave labor; it was a strange cauldron of greed, wealth, discord, misery, and bondage. At the dawn of the revolution in 1789, the society contained three major social classes: the White colonists totaling approximately 40,000; the African slaves ranging anywhere from 500,000 to 700,000 (depending on which estimates one looks at); and a third class known as the *Affranchis* or *gens de couleur*, referring primarily to the offspring of a White master and a *négresse*. There were approximately 28,000 *Affranchis*. All throughout colonial history inter- and intragroup conflicts were commonplace. Within these groups, there were conflicts of interests and fragmentation that were threatening the seeming opulence of the society and tearing apart the economic and social systems on which this opulence rested. Indeed, observers of colonial Saint-Domingue had long warned that "this colony of slaves is like a city under the imminence of attack; we are treading on loaded barrels of gunpowder."[10] The Saint-Domingue revolution that broke out in 1791 proved them right.

CONTEXT OF THE REVOLUTION

The Saint-Domingue revolution is perhaps the most significant component of Haitian history, and as such it has received the greatest amount of coverage.[11] In this section, a succinct description of the three major social classes of colonial Saint-Domingue is offered, as they represent the social and economic structure that explains the primary causes of the revolution.[12]

Whites

The White class included three distinct groups differentiated by their power, capital, and ownership of the land and of the slaves: the *grands blancs* (big Whites), les *couches moyennes* (the middle class), and the *petits blancs* (small Whites). The first group comprised colonial officials (the governor and high-ranking representatives of the metropolitan political apparatus and trade cartels), whose duties were to ensure that the main purpose of the colony of Saint-Domingue was to loyally serve the metropolis and "enrich the mother country by providing a market for its surplus products, a home for its surplus population and a source of cheap raw materials."[13] Also included in the group of *grands blancs* were the rich planters who owned the lucrative sugar plantations and most of the slaves. The colonial officials and the rich planters, often tied together by kinship and marriage, held the reins of power and influence in colonial Saint-Domingue. A significant number of these planters did not have permanent homes in the colony; they preferred to live in France, enjoying the luxuries and comforts that their Saint-Domingue investments ensured them. These absentee landlords left their estates and plantations in the care of plantation managers or *procureurs* (overseers). The second group, the *couches moyennes,* or the middle class, was composed mostly of these overseers and of the owners of the indigo, cotton, and coffee plantations, which were smaller and required less capital than the sugar plantations. In addition, this class included members of the liberal professions, self-employed artisans, technicians, and petty local bureaucrats. This group consisted of a more or less privileged section of the White population. Indeed, plantation owners had slaves, and the overseers not only were in complete control of the administration of the plantations and assumed all the rights and prerogatives of the owners but also could become plantation owners themselves. Finally, the third group, the *petits blancs* (small Whites) included shopkeepers, retail merchants, grocers, unskilled artisans, craftsmen, and "whole hosts of vagabonds, petty criminals, debtors, and soldiers-of-fortune who swarmed to Saint-Domingue."[14] The *petits blancs* were landless and were at the very bottom of the White social pyramid. They were among the most racist elements of Saint-Domingue and they harbored strong feelings of resentment against the *grands blancs* and the *Affranchis* (freedmen), with whom they competed for employment opportunities.

Conflicts of interest existed within the White population. The *grands blancs,* particularly the large planters, were angry at the French mercantile policy, which specifically stated that "the colonies are founded by and for the Metropolis." They were tired of sending their profits to the metropolis and of paying the very high taxes it levied on the colony. They wanted a certain degree of free trade, particularly with rival Britain and the United States; they aspired to break away from France altogether. The *petits blancs,* themselves, were not keen on the idea of severing all ties with France for fear they would be under the unbridled domination of colonial aristocracy.[15] As for the middle class, the position of its members varied according to the degree of wealth: the more privileged members allied themselves with the separatist ideology of the elite; the less privileged joined the cause of the small Whites. The interests and aspirations of the various groups of Whites determined their relationships with the other two social classes present in Saint-Domingue, namely the *Affranchis* and the slaves.

Affranchis

The *Affranchis* or free coloreds were mostly Mulattoes. In the context of colonial Saint-Domingue, a Mulatto can be defined as the offspring of French fathers and Black slave mothers. By genetic makeup, a Mulatto is a hybrid product. Many of these Mulattoes were freed by their fathers and sent to France for their education. These Mulattoes, called *Affranchis* or *gens de couleur,* considered themselves to be Frenchpersons of color, and many of them managed to prosper and acquire capital, estates, and slaves. It is reported that they were among the leading coffee growers of the colony. Some also had good positions in commerce and trade. In general, the Mulatto *Affranchis* fared relatively well, and it is said that some were so rich that they could imitate the lifestyle of the Whites. One scholar reports that the "*affranchis* owned one-third of the plantation property, one-quarter of the slaves, and one-quarter of the real estate property in Saint Domingue.... Circumstances permitting, a few had even 'infiltrated' the almost exclusively *grand blanc* domain of the sugar plantation by becoming managers of the paternal estate upon the father's return to Europe or even inheritors of property upon the father's death."[16] The same scholar also informs us that by 1763, at least three hundred White planters were married to *Affranchi* women in Saint-Domingue.

So, this group of privileged Mulattoes had good reason to aspire to complete parity with the Whites.

The *Affranchi* class, in addition to the Mulattoes, also included some Blacks who were free because they had bought or earned their freedom thanks to "faithful or extraordinary service."[17] One of the many contradictions of the colonial system was that some slaves were allowed to cultivate small garden plots. Planters who wanted to free themselves from the burden of feeding their slaves allotted them small plots to grow their own subsistence crops on Sundays and holidays. Besides producing food crops, some of these slaves made handicrafts that they were allowed to sell along with the small surplus from their gardens. The income generated from these transactions enabled them to buy their freedom; thus, through manumission, a limited number of them passed from slave status to *Affranchi* status. Most the Black *Affranchis* were artisans, and their status was inferior to that of the Mulatto *Affranchis* who were plantation owners and owned slaves. In the words of one scholar, "the Mulatto *Affranchi* despised the Black *Affranchi*."[18]

Among the *Affranchi* population, the Mulattoes were the overwhelming majority. However, in spite of the fact that many owned property and slaves and were part of a more or less privileged segment of colonial society, they were increasingly the object of discriminatory regulations on the part of the White establishment, who saw in them a threat to racial hegemony in the colony and, by ricochet, to the maintenance of slavery. Whites reasoned that only through repressive social legislation could they maintain their social and economic privileges against the so-called encroachments of the *Affranchis*.[19] Consequently, free coloreds in Saint-Domingue, regardless of their slave- and property-owner status, were prohibited from exercising certain professions, such as the priesthood, law, pharmacy, or medicine, and from holding any public office. Moreover, they were excluded from officers' ranks within the military and were required to pay taxes that Whites did not have to pay. An *Affranchi* also could not eat at a table with a White. In colonial Saint-Domingue, property ownership and freedom were not sufficient conditions to get access to power and political privileges. Race was the sine qua non condition for supremacy and membership in the colonial ruling class. To maintain their supremacy, the exclusion of the *gens de couleur* from certain prestigious activities was an imperative.

However, in spite of the restrictions against the social and political advancement of the *Affranchis,* there were some flagrant contradictions. First, they could bear arms in order to defend the interests of the Whites. In fact, they were encouraged to join the *maréchaussée,* a local law-enforcement unit composed exclusively of *Affranchis,* created for the sole purpose of hunting down runaway slaves. Furthermore, when France sent an expeditionary force to help American patriots fight the British, this force included a Mulatto contingent from Saint-Domingue, known as the *chasseurs volontaires de couleur* (as can be recalled from chapter 1). Mulattoes were exposed to the idea of revolution under the claim of liberty. Moreover, those who had been to France for their education knew quite well the revolutionary slogan, *liberté, égalité, fraternité.*

In sum, the Mulatto *Affranchis* always constituted an ambivalent interest and status group: On the one hand, they were at odds and at war with the Whites with whom they aspired to full political equality, and they were tired of being considered second-class citizens. On the other hand, they allied themselves with the Whites in their desire to maintain slavery and voiced the argument that colonial economy would be unworkable without it. Moreover, they believed that because of their color, Blacks were doomed to servitude. One must not forget that the Mulattoes owned as many as one-quarter of the slaves in the colony, and because of this, they had a common interest with the Whites, which was the preservation of property and of the slavery system. However, the continuous vexations and denial of equal rights they suffered at the hands of the Whites would cause a shift in their allegiance. This shift was further triggered by the brutal execution of two of their leaders (along with several of their followers), Vincent Ogé and Jean-Baptiste Chavannes in February 1791 (the latter was one of the *chasseurs volontaires de couleur* who participated in the Battle of Savannah). By the time of the revolution, they sided with the Blacks to create a Saint-Domingue or a Haiti without the French, where they could ultimately become the real masters.

Slaves

The largest segment of the total population of Saint-Domingue was the slaves. Those brought from Africa were known as the *nègres bossals* (primitive slaves, to be understood as uncivilized), and those born from slave parents in the colony were the *nègres créoles* (to be understood as more civilized). The *bossals* were significantly more numerous than the *créoles,* since the horror of slave life—which considerably raised mortality rates, as well as sterility among women—prevented the slaves from replenishing their numbers by reproduction. Consequently, this required the constant influx of fresh supplies of slaves. According to one estimate, two-thirds of the slaves in Saint-Domingue were *bossal.* Most of the *bossal* slaves worked on the plantations under the supervision of a *nègre commandeur* (slave driver). In most cases, the slave driver was either a créole slave who had superior knowledge of the environment and of colonial life or a former *bossal* slave who had the same qualifications as the former. Later on, these *nègres commandeurs* would play a critical role in the mobilization of slaves to join the revolution. The greater number of *créole* slaves worked in the masters' residences as servants, and some were artisan slaves. Through manumission, several were able to buy their freedom. Toussaint Louverture, who would become the most prominent leader of the Saint-Domingue revolution as will be discussed later, belonged to this supposedly more privileged category of *nègres*.[20] From his father, who was also a privileged slave owing to his knowledge of medicinal plants, Toussaint learned the trade and served as his master's coachman and, ultimately, as steward of all the livestock of the estate.

Most accounts indicate that "by far the most intense utilization of slaves' labor was on the sugar plantations, where, during the harvest and grinding season, an ordinary workday could easily average eighteen to twenty hours."[21] However, it is also reported that the rhythm of production was no less arduous on the coffee plantations situated on mountainous slopes where the climate was cooler and the rains more frequent. "Ill-protected against the evening and night chill with inadequate clothing, ill-fed, undernourished, and overworked, the slaves on the coffee plantations suffered a mortality rate that was exceedingly high."[22] Moreover, "punishment, often surpassing the human imagination in its grotesque refinements of barbarism and torture, was often the order of the day."[23] Needless to say, the slaves ultimately revolted against the brutality and the dehumanization of the colonial system and wanted to free themselves forever from the yoke of their masters. Their resistance, which culminated in the 1791 revolution, took many forms all throughout a century of bondage.

Of the many forms of slave resistance, the most successful was the *marronage*. Large numbers of bold slaves who could no longer endure the atrocities of slavery escaped to the forests and the mountains and set up resistance communities in the mountainous interior of the island. In 1720, 1,000 slaves fled to the mountains; in 1751, there were at least 3,000 of them. These slaves, known as *marrons,* continuously raided and burned the plantations of the masters. Soon, they constituted a real danger to the colonial establishment, which created a unit known as the *maréchaussée,* composed of *Affranchis* as discussed earlier, to hunt them down. However, in spite of these efforts, marronage could never be suppressed, and it became a structure of organized Black resistance against Whites. Leaders emerged among the various maroon communities that could unite and organize them. One such leader was Mackandal, who in the 1750s attempted (unsuccessfully) the first structured slave uprising movement in Saint-Domingue, some forty years before the events of 1791. He was eventually captured in January 1758 and burned at the stake. However, Mackandal's death did not deter slave resistance. Revolts, conspiracies, poisoning, and marronage reached even greater proportions. Slave consciousness solidified, as maroon slaves continued to successfully spread the idea of freedom to the entire class of Blacks held in bondage. From slave to slave, from plantation to plantation, the concept of *liberté* was ringing louder and louder. Slave consciousness reached its peak on the night of August 14, 1791, when slaves in the north attended a ceremony held in Bois-Caïman, not very far from the city of Cap-Haitian. The ceremony was presided over by a *gros nègre* named Boukman, who, by all accounts, was both a *nègre commandeur* who exerted a great deal of power and influence over his slaves and a Vodou priest, or *oungan*. This ceremony was organized to set the final date and detail for the massive slave insurrection that would begin on the night of August 22, 1791.

To summarize, on the eve of the revolution in August 1791, Saint-Domingue was a volcano about to erupt. It was a place totally fragmented by the clash of interests within the different factions of colonial society. The *grands blancs* were pressing their claims for greater autonomy for the colony—which entailed free trade—and they were demanding the right to decide colonial affairs by raising "the principle of national self-determination."[24] The *petits blancs* resented the *grands blancs* and, in general, tended to respond more favorably to colonywide policies and trends set up by the metropolis. The Mulatto *Affranchis,* who were asserting their own interests against those of the colonial aristocracy, demanded equality with Whites. The slaves, in retaliation for the atrocities of a century of slavery, were fomenting a bloody revolt and were mobilizing themselves as a revolutionary force. In the meantime, France was fighting its own revolution, to the delight of its rivals, Great Britain and Spain. The ideals embedded in the revolutionary motto—*liberté, égalité, fraternité*—resounded forcefully in the colony. Separation from the mother country became the motto of the large planters, *égalité* with Whites that of the Mulattoes, and *liberté* that of the slaves. To complicate matters, by 1793 war broke out in Europe; England and Spain were at odds with France and were threatening to seize (and had begun invading) the prosperous colony of Saint-Domingue. Let us not forget that the British, because they had already lost to American patriots, had good reason to want to take control of Saint-Domingue, the finest colony of the Americas. In a similar vein, the Spanish who occupied the eastern two-thirds of the island wanted to weaken the French and recover from them what had been part of Spain's first American colony. Consequently, they welcomed maroon slaves within their ranks to fight against the French forces. In short, Saint-Domingue was in complete turmoil and chaos.

THE SAINT-DOMINGUE REVOLUTION AND INDEPENDENCE

On the night of August 22, 1791, the 12-year bloody revolution of Saint-Domingue began. Armed with pruning hooks, machetes, and torches, angry slaves burned estates and plantations and slaughtered White colonists. In spite of repressive measures by the White establishment to attempt to crush the uprising, it could not be suppressed and the destruction of plantations spread to other regions of the island, namely the west and the south. As one scholar remarks, "the planters did not have a chance against the pent-up fury of half a million slaves."[25] The insurrection had reached the point of no return. The capture of Boukman did not stop the slaves; other well-known leaders—Jean-François, Biassou, Toussaint Louverture, and Jean-Jacques Dessalines—emerged. The Mulattoes joined the revolution, under the leadership of André Rigaud (who was also a *chasseur volontaire de couleur* at the Battle of Savannah). At this point, both groups seemed to have been united to fight the common enemy: the French.

The French were losing ground fast: Many had already been killed; some of the lucky ones fled for their lives. Moreover, the Spanish next door continued to lure the slaves by making them soldiers of the armies of the king of Spain. Toussaint Louverture joined the Spanish army and received the official title of general; he called for the support of his men because he believed that an alliance with Spain would ensure freedom for the slaves. France had to send two civil commissions to Saint-Domingue, one in 1791 and another one in 1792, in an attempt to ease this volatile situation. In order to safeguard the colony, the French commissioners were prepared to make radical concessions: They granted full civil and political rights to all freed Mulattoes who were already defending their claims by the force of arms. Additionally, they started modifying the status of the slaves to stop them from going over to the Spanish. They went as far as to decree that "all slaves who joined the French army would be freed and granted full equality with whites and people of color."[26] Finally, Sonthonax, one the civil French commissioners, declared slavery abolished in Saint-Domingue in August 1793. By the time the French government was forced to make these concessions, many of the most lucrative plantations were destroyed and rendered nonfunctional. In addition, the Mulattoes had taken arms against the Whites who had refused to accept the decree issued by the French civil commissioners, and they were bloodily clamoring for equality. The British and Spanish were making headway to retrieve whatever they thought could be restored to them of the colony.

Subsequently, in 1794, Toussaint Louverture shifted his allegiance to the French and demanded "the full and unequivocal declaration of the emancipation of the slaves by the French government, and not just by its civil commissioners."[27] He joined the French army as brigadier general and fought within its ranks against the British and the Spanish. After a long struggle, the former withdrew from Saint-Domingue in November 1798; the latter were defeated by Toussaint and his troops when they occupied the Spanish city of Santo Domingo in January 1801. Soon after this military victory, Toussaint drafted a constitution in which he proclaimed himself governor-for-life of the French island of Saint-Domingue (May 1801). Governor Louverture and his army of ex-slaves had indeed become a political force in Saint-Domingue. Napoleon Bonaparte was not prepared to accept the autonomy of Saint-Domingue, nor was he willing to recognize the rise of a Black governor acting on his own initiative. He was determined to reimpose absolute metropolitan control and to return the so-called gilded Africans to where they belonged: the plantations (as slaves, of course).

In November and December 1801, the French emperor sent a massive naval force to Saint-Domingue under the command of his brother-in-law, Admiral Leclerc. Toussaint was eventually captured and exiled in June 1802; as he stepped aboard the ship that was taking him to France, he spoke those famous prophetic words reported in every history book about the Haitian revolution:

> In overthrowing me, you have cut down only the trunk of the tree of liberty in Saint-Domingue. It will spring up again by the roots, for they are numerous and deep.

Toussaint was imprisoned in the Fort-de-Joux, situated in the Jura Mountains, where he died on April 7, 1803.

Subsequently, the atrocities committed by the French troops against the Blacks and the Mulattoes, as well as the dread of reenslavement, solidified the unity and alliance of these two groups. At this time, there was no doubt that their freedom was in danger. The Mulattoes, under the leadership of Alexandre Pétion, joined the Blacks, led by Jean-Jacques Dessalines, and all were driven by the burning desire to defeat the French at all costs. On May 18, 1803, they decided to get rid of the French flag, and they united themselves under their own Black flag; they also swore allegiance to Dessalines. Driven by the rallying war cry of their leader, *koupe tèt, boule kay* (cut off heads, and burn houses), they defeated the French army, already weakened by yellow fever, at the historic battle of Vertierres (near Cap-Haitian) in November

1803. France had lost forever its pearl of the Antilles. The revolution begun by Mackandal and Boukman was won, the vision and prophecy of Toussaint Louverture realized. On January 1, 1804, the declaration of independence was formally proclaimed: Saint-Domingue had ceased to exist; a new nation of Blacks was born, masters of the land of Haiti, as the country was now renamed.

CONCLUSION

This brief overview of the colonial period leading to independence enables us to understand why Haitians are so proud of their past, and why they take this glorious past with them wherever they migrate. Indeed, from Quisqueya to Saint-Domingue to Haiti, the Haitian people have come a long way in forging their own destiny. January 1, 1804, is their finest hour, for it symbolizes the end

Young Haitian woman displays the colors of the Haitian Flag at the *Konpa* Festival at Bayfront Park in Miami in May of 2003. Courtesy of the *Haitian Times*.

of bondage, the end of White supremacy, and their right to be a sovereign nation. It is therefore not by accident that this date has come to be the most celebrated by Haitians everywhere. Haitians in the United States are no exceptions. For example, in Boston, the Haitian Independence Gala (as was mentioned at the beginning of the chapter) is a well established event that seeks to acknowledge Haiti's leading role in the Black freedom movement around the world, in its capacity of the first Black republic. Haitian Flag's Day, on May 18, is another date that Haitian Americans choose to recognize, and the reason for that choice is now evident. In schools with large numbers of Haitian students, particularly in New York and Miami, this day takes on particular significance, as many activities are organized to inform the entire school population that Haitian students, too, have a rich history filled with great achievements. Behind all the celebrations and recognitions, the message seems to be clear: the Haitian American experience, deeply rooted in Haitian history, is a significant component of the great American odyssey. Moreover, as is explained in chapter 3, a great deal of Haitian history is intertwined with U.S. foreign policies.

Haitian children attending Catholic mass at St. Agnes Cathedral in Rockville Centre in Rockland County, NY, to celebrate Haitian Flag Day. Courtesy of the *Haitian Times*.

NOTES

1. I am indebted to Charlot Lucien, a member of the Haitian Heritage Month Advisory Committee, for providing me with the text of Senator Owens's remarks.

2. The full text of Governor Pataki's proclamation was posted on the New York Haitian Consulate's Web site.

3. As quoted in Heinl, Heinl, and Heinl (1995: 14).

4. Rogozinski (1999: 29).

5. Ibid., pp. 38, 85.

6. Dantès Bellegarde from his 1938 work, *La Nation Haïtienne,* as reproduced in Arthur and Dash (1999: 25–26).

7. As reported in Heinl, Heinl, and Heinl (1995: 24).

8. Ibid., p. 31.

9. Ibid., p. 35.

10. Ibid.

11. Among the several works on the Haitian Revolution, C. L. R. James's book *The Black Jacobins* is a classic. Other important works include Dupuy (1989), Fick (1990), Trouillot (1990), Geggus (2002), and Heinl, Heinl, and Heinl (1995).

12. The following pages are in part based on updated sections of a previous work (Zéphir 1996: 26–33).

13. Nicholls (1996: 22).

14. Fick (1990: 17).

15. Nicholls (1996: 22).

16. Fick (1990: 19–20).

17. Weinstein and Segal (1992: 17).

18. Moreau de Saint-Méry (1958: 102).

19. Fick (1990: 20).

20. Geggus (2002: 37) asserts that Toussaint was free since at least the mid-1770s.

21. Fick (1990: 28).

22. Ibid., p. 29.

23. Ibid., p. 34.

24. Dupuy (1989: 47).

25. Dash (2001: 5).

26. Dupuy (1989: 49).

27. Ibid., p. 44.

3

Haiti: The Making of a Nation

January 1, 1804, marks the birth of Haiti as the first Black republic of the world, and the second independent republic of the Western Hemisphere (after the United States). From that moment henceforth, the fragile nation, composed of a multitude of slaves liberated by the violence of bloodshed, faced Herculean challenges: Would it be accepted by the world powers as a sovereign nation? How would it erase class conflicts inherited from the colonial regime? How would it manage its newly won freedom? How would it learn to govern itself? How would it restore the agricultural economy destroyed by years of revolution? What new institutions would it create? Would it be able to prosper and afford its citizens the basic commodities of life? This chapter explores all these questions and demonstrates that, from the start, the new nation was not able to overcome these monumental challenges. Over the course of two centuries, from 1804 through the present day, the country never recovered from the legacy of slavery and its aftermath. Isolation, neglect, corruption, greed, dictatorship, political and economic instability, and poverty have plagued the country and have affected the lives of many Haitians to the point that migration to more attractive shores, such as the United States, became their only recourse. The following pages attempt to underscore and analyze the salient problems encountered by the Haitian nation, problems whose roots can be traced back to the early independence period, in an attempt to inform readers of the conditions that compel so many Haitians to seek greener pastures in foreign lands.

THE SOCIOECONOMIC LEGACY
OF THE REVOLUTION

The revolution left the new nation in a state of great economic disruption. Twelve years of civil and foreign war (particularly with Spain and Great Britain) had taken a very heavy toll on Haiti, both with regard to material and human losses. Further, in the aftermath of independence, Dessalines, who just like Toussaint had proclaimed himself governor-general-for-life and later emperor, ordered the slaughter of all French who were still in the country. In his view, Haiti had to be cleansed of every French taint. More destruction and carnage was to come in the early part of 1804.

After his cleansing operation, Dessalines was faced with the colossal task of building the new nation from ruins and ashes. Additionally, he was confronted with other serious problems: Who would control the new government, and who would own the land? The Blacks or the Mulattoes? Although independence was won under the alliance between the Mulattoes and Blacks, Dessalines never fully trusted these Mulattoes who, after all, were descendents from Frenchmen and who, as landowners, had owned Black slaves. From the start, the new nation was divided along color lines and ownership of the land. Blacks and Mulattoes disagreed fundamentally on two issues: politics and land distribution. In a climate of mistrust and discord, Dessalines was assassinated on October 17, 1806.

After Dessalines's death, the country became totally divided between two camps, the Mulattoes in the west and the south headed by Pétion, and the Blacks in the north headed by Christophe. Pétion, who was elected president in March 1807, could not defeat the northern armies; therefore, he became factional president until his death from malaria in March 1818. From January 1807 to October 1820 (when he committed suicide), the northern region remained under the reign of Christophe, who in March 1811 crowned himself King Henry I. Consequently, 14 years of civil war began, and the economic situation of the country (already in lamentable shape after the revolution) further deteriorated; production dropped, and growth ceased. Neither Pétion nor Christophe did much to halt the decline. After Christophe put a silver bullet in his head on October 20, 1820, the southern troops under the leadership of Boyer, who became president after Pétion's death, marched to Cap-Haitian; the north was finally won and reunited with the republic. Boyer ruled the country until 1843. By then it had become clear that Haiti could not build a viable agrarian economy from the ruined plantation system. Boyer continued Pétion's practice of granting small parcels of land to the peasantry and to members of the army. Observers of that period claimed that Haiti was in ruins and that sugar export had ceased. The country was definitely not on a path to recovery.

In short, the socioeconomic legacy of the revolution was that the country was in complete ruins and chaos. The agrarian system was nonfunctional and the country was divided between the army and the peasants and between a Mulatto and a Black elite. In the words of one scholar, Haitian politics in the postindependence era can be described as follows: "Intrigue, conspiracy, treachery, violence, coups, caste against caste, color against color, region against region."[1]

These conditions would prevail all throughout nineteenth-century Haiti, and well into the twentieth century. The period from 1843 through the U.S. occupation in 1915 witnessed even greater deterioration. In that 72-year period, a military elite came to power, which paid little attention to agricultural economy, preferring to become involved in the ruthless pursuit of political power. During this period of great political confusion, 22 heads of state held the reins of government, all of them military men. Of that number, 14 were overthrown by insurrections and 3 killed in office. As another scholar observed, "changes in head of state, constitutional crises, revolution and counterrevolution were the surface manifestations of a socioeconomic system in crisis."[2] The decisions and policies of the early leaders, which themselves can be explained by the realities of their times as was described in some detail, shaped the direction of the country for centuries to come. The fear of a French (or other power's) invasion compelled heads of state of the time to put too much weight into the army, at the neglect of the masses of the people. The overmilitarization of the country is felt to the present day. From independence henceforth, the socioeconomic system remained in crisis, and the country never erased class conflicts inherited from the colonial regime and the early years of independence. It never really prospered and never afforded *all* its citizens the basic commodities of life. Political instability permeated and still permeates the Haitian context. A measure of this can be found in the fact that from 1804 to 2002, Haiti has been ruled by 37 presidents, from Dessalines to Aristide—some lasting several years, while others were exiled or killed in office after serving only a few months—and 7 military juntas (the first in 1946; and the latest 3 succeeding each other at less than one-year intervals, from 1986 to 1988, right after the overthrow of Jean-Claude "Baby Doc" Duvalier).

HAITI'S LACK OF RECOGNITION
AFTER INDEPENDENCE

After its independence, the new nation faced another great challenge: that of its recognition as a sovereign nation by the world powers. Some Haitian historians have explained the actions of the leaders of the independence era by the refusal of powerful nations to acknowledge Haiti's independence. According to their point of view, the Haitian revolutionary leaders, driven by the desire to have their country recognized as a full-fledged nation, began to give themselves titles comparable to those of rulers of France, Great Britain, and Spain. Indeed, immediately after Napoleon Bonaparte crowned himself emperor, Dessalines followed suit. Christophe did the same thing when be proclaimed himself King Henry I and built a series of extravagant palaces. After all, this was what European monarchs did. In 1849, another president, by the name of Faustin Soulouque, followed this tradition when he proclaimed himself emperor of Haiti. By attempting to emulate such behaviors in search of recognition, these Haitian heads of state distanced themselves from the masses of the people, who by then had become their subjects, maintained in servile conditions. These actions did not achieve their desired results, as Haiti remained ostracized by the world. The existence of independent Haiti, because it gave hope to the other Blacks still in slavery in the New World, constituted a warning and a threat to the European powers and to the slave owners of the United States. As one scholar observed, "the specter of a free Negro republic that owed its independence to a successful slave revolt frightened slaveholding countries as much as the shadow of the Bolshevist Russia alarmed capitalist countries in 1917."[3] The United States put an embargo on commerce with Haiti in February of 1806. Haiti's recognition by the world would not occur until it "regularized" its relationship with the former metropolis. In 1825, France agreed to conditionally accept Haiti's independence, providing that the Haitian government paid the French government an indemnity of 150 million francs over five years—115 million francs for the former colonial plantation owners and 35 million francs to the French government for colonial buildings and fortifications, all in ruins by 1825. In order to lift all embargos, which would allow Haiti to trade with other nations, President Boyer agreed to pay this indemnity along with the imposed high interests. In consequence, to make the payments, he began to deplete the country's liquid reserves and to borrow money from French capitalists themselves. To add insult to injury, following the French example, Germany, Great Britain, and the United States also asked for financial reparations for their nationals who lost either their lives or their properties during the revolution or after independence. In order to keep up with the interest payments, successive Haitian governments were compelled to depend on loans from French, German, British, and U.S. bankers. It is estimated that the repayment of these loans consumed approximately 80 percent of the national revenue by the end of the nineteenth century.[4] From the beginning of its national history, Haiti became involved in an endless cycle of debts and loans that persists to the present day. In short, the heavy indemnities that Haiti was forced to pay to powerful nations in return for recognition and an end to its isolation from global markets contributed greatly to bankrupting the country, in addition, of course, to the greed and corruption of its own heads of state, as was explained above. Perhaps, the answer to the question often asked by many—Why is Haiti, which once was the pearl of the Antilles, so poor?—is getting more evident.

THE U.S. OCCUPATION OF HAITI

The acute political and economic instability of the country, particularly during 1911 and 1915 when six presidents succeeded one another in office, culminating with the lynching of the last one, provided the United States with a great motive to invade Haiti. In the face of economic ruin, the Haitian elite relied on heavy borrowings from foreign powers, particularly France, Germany, and the United States; in consequence, the country was already falling into the hands of its foreign creditors. At the dawn of the U.S. occupation, there were significant numbers of foreign investors and merchants in Haiti, German in particular. American investors were eagerly looking for ways to have the monopoly of investments in the country. In fact, by 1910, it is said that U.S. bankers controlled the National Bank of Haiti. It is also said that some members of the Mulatto elite asked the United States to intervene to restore stability.[5] Therefore, financial conditions existed for more U.S. control of Haiti. Moreover, the United States, all along, had always wanted to secure a naval base in the Caribbean, and with the completion of the Panama Canal in sight, it had become all the more important for the Americans to obtain such a base and to prevent any further European penetration of the Caribbean. Since the establishment of the Monroe Doctrine and later the Roosevelt Corollary, gaining absolute control of the Caribbean region became a fundamental principle of U.S. foreign policy; and, by all means, Europe, by then embroiled in Word War I, had to be kept out of the hemisphere. Both financial interests and strategic factors weighted heavily in the U.S. decision to occupy Haiti. On July 29, 1915, the U.S. Marines landed in Port-au-Prince, and a 19-year U.S. occupation began.

Political reorganization started immediately during the summer of 1915. In essence, the United States sought the support of the Mulatto elite, believing that this group would be very favorable to U.S. investment in Haiti. In the words of one scholar, "the Americans, then, aimed to make Haiti a stable and subservient neighbour and a safe field for investment."[6] The occupation put an end to the financial hold of German and French businessmen alike, as the United States decided to help Haiti consolidate its foreign debts, thus ensuring the monopoly of U.S. capitalists, a monopoly that endures to this day. As a direct result of this dollar diplomacy policy, U.S. investment in Haiti tripled between 1915 and 1930. In the words of one observer, "occupation financial policy, like most facets of the occupation, looked first to American interests."[7] A new constitution was drafted in 1918, allowing foreigners to own land in Haiti. Under the new constitution, U.S. companies acquired large amounts of land for agricultural projects. It is believed that in the north alone, "50,000 Haitians were expropriated."[8]

Furthermore, the U.S. troops right away began training a new Haitian armed force, called the *gendarmerie* (later renamed *Garde d'Haïti*), disbanding the old military, which was the continuation of the revolutionary model. The senior posts of this *gendarmerie* were occupied at first by the U.S. Marines, until the full "haitianization" of this force was complete in 1934 by the end of the occupation. In the minds of U.S. troops, a well-trained armed force was necessary to crush any opposition to current governments (particularly Mulatto governments) and to the U.S. occupation itself. Moreover, the United States reasoned that it was essential to have the Haitian army in place with the "right" compliant government, after the marines' departure, in order to maintain political order and stability, necessary to its own financial and geographic interests. Part of the political instability of the preoccupation period was due to the fact that for many years (since the 1860s) the Black peasantry had organized itself as a structured movement called the *Cacos* to fight the abuses committed by the elite and the soldiers. In fact, these *Cacos* mounted a resistance against the U.S. occupation, which ended in the killing of their leader Charlemagne Péralte by U.S. troops in October 1919. Around the same time as the Haitian *gendarmerie* was created, the U.S. troops forced Haitian peasants to work under an ancient labor regimen known as *corvée* (instituted during colonial times, and revived in 1863 by Haitian president Geffrard). This system required the inhabitants to work on road building and other public works projects throughout the country away from their homes and families, under the armed supervision of the *blancs* (U.S. soldiers) and the newly trained Haitian *gendarmes,* with nominal pay and inadequate food and lodging.[9] These *gendarmes* quite often resorted to brutal methods to obtain submission. This system of forced labor led to growing resentment, and the workers believed the *blancs* had come to restore slavery. Moreover, the U.S. Marines centralized all state power in Port-au-Prince. Economic and military centralization allowed Americans to maintain greater control over the affairs of the country. The construction of roads leading to the capital was undertaken to facilitate their centralization efforts. The devastating consequences of these measures, particularly the allocation of a great amount of power to the *gendarmerie,* are still felt in present-day Haiti. The Americans made advances in the material rehabilitation of the country, as evidenced in the construction of buildings and roads and the establishment of vocational schools (such as the agricultural college of Damiens that still exists today) and a telephone system, but they did not lay the foundations of democracy in Haiti. The armed forces and the presidents they left behind never served the interests of the people. On the contrary, they plundered the public treasury to enrich themselves as rapidly as they could, while oppressing the masses. This nondemocratic state of affairs has characterized Haiti all throughout the years and still represents contemporary conditions; it is at the root of Haiti's current abject poverty and insecure political climate. Indeed, the amount of abuse and persecution countless numbers of Haitians have experienced at the hands of the army has been well documented in media in the United States and around the world. Those conditions undoubtedly explain the genesis of Haitian migration. There is evidence to document that the Haitian exodus to other shores began during the U.S. occupation: large numbers of dispossessed Haitian peasants went to the Dominican Republic (to be killed later in 1937 by the Trujillo regime); other Black intellectuals went to Latin America acques Roumain, for example, who went to Mexico) and the United States, where they settled primarily in Harlem. Approximately two hundred Haitians migrated to this country during the occupation.

In 1934, the U.S. troops, having accomplished their goals—centralization of state power, establishment of an armed force, complicity of the Mulatto elite, monopoly of U.S. investors, and securing a base in the Caribbean—departed. However, things did not remain stable; eventually, a new Black nationalist ideology, the *noirisme,* began to develop, as members of the Black elite were getting fed up with the authoritarian policies of the Mulattoes, along with their disdain for the Blacks. This ideology gained some popularity, as it strongly argued that the country needed to regain its dignity after the humiliations of the U.S. occupation (to be understood as White occupation). In 1946, with the support of the military, a Black president (Dumarsais Estimé) was brought to power and a Black middle class emerged. It is the same *noiriste* current that brought François "Papa Doc" Duvalier to the presidency in 1957. Haiti had entered the duvalierist era, which unfortunately was to bring more bloodshed and more misery to the people for another 30 years.

THE DUVALIER ERA: "PAPA DOC"

Duvalier's presidency is accurately described in the literature as a dictatorship. As one scholar puts it, the extreme nature of his government makes it "the most disturbing manifestation of state power in Haitian history."[10] Duvalier's first order of business was to arrest or to exile his political opponents and their supporters and to purge the Haitian army in fear of military coups, as he was well aware of its power and its role in political affairs. Duvalier reorganized the military by creating his own personal army, known as the *Garde Présidentielle,* within the armed forces. Moreover, Duvalier did not stop there; he created another civilian militia force, known as the *Tontons Macoutes,* as a countervailing force to keep the army under control. These Macoutes were drawn from a wide cross-section of Haitian society, "providing a network of intelligence gathering and nationwide intimidation of any potential opposition."[11] Duvalier also dismantled all the civil institutions that could potentially pose a threat to his regime. Schools, churches, trade unions, universities, as well as the media were undermined, as teachers, intellectuals, and priests were forced into exile and journalists and other civilians tortured and killed. Duvalier established a regime of sheer terror to keep him in power, and according to a report by Amnesty International (February 1978), the mortality rate of political prisoners during the Duvalier era was the highest in the world. In addition to keeping the army in check and eliminating real or imagined sources of opposition, Duvalier also decided to do something about the Mulatto elite who, during the presidential election of 1957, had supported his Mulatto rival, Louis Déjoie. Moreover, in the early years of his presidency, there had been a couple of failed attempts on the part of exiled Mulatto army officers to overthrow him. Therefore, Duvalier felt he had ample reason to deal with the Mulatto class once and for all. He ordered the slaughter of entire Mulatto families living predominantly in the southern city of Jérémie. The execution of these families—from babies to the paralyzed elderly—in 1964 by the Tontons Macoutes is one of the many horrific chapters of the Duvalier agenda. It is said that after the butchery bodies were left to rot in public view. By 1964, duvalierism had prevailed: the dictator had stamped out his internal enemies and rivals, fended off invasions, dismantled trade unions, and expelled progressive Catholic priests. To complete his ascension, Duvalier proclaimed himself president-for-life, with the power to designate his successor. Terror and repression were his tactics; little attention was paid to the economic welfare of the country. In fact, the public treasury was siphoned and foreign aid diverted to pay off supporters, Macoutes, and high-ranking administrators. It is believed that Papa Doc's 14 long years of dictatorship claimed the lives of tens of thousands of Haitians.

For many Haitians, migration became the only way to flee the atrocities committed by Duvalier's Tontons Macoutes. The Immigration and Naturalization Service documents that 34,499 Haitians migrated legally to the United States between 1961 and 1970, a period that coincided precisely with the François Duvalier era. It is reported that by the mid-1960s, 80 percent of Haiti's qualified professionals—doctors, lawyers, teachers, engineers, and public administrators—left the country and relocated to places like New York and Montreal. Another report states that "by 1970, there were more Haitian physicians in either Montreal or New York than in Haiti."[12] Gradually, large colonies of Haitians outside of Haiti were forming, colonies that would eventually constitute a solid Haitian diaspora in the United States, impacting its social, economic, and political landscape, as will be discussed in forthcoming chapters.

THE DUVALIER ERA: "BABY DOC"

In January of 1971, a debilitated and enfeebled Papa Doc announced that his son Jean-Claude Duvalier would be his successor. On April 22, 1971 (less than 24 hours after the death of his father, which occurred in the evening hours of April 21), the 19-year-old Baby Doc was sworn in. Most accounts suggest that there was on the surface a relaxation in the use of state power and a toning down of the noiriste ideology during Jean-Claude Duvalier's reign. The new president claimed that he was more concerned with the "economic revolution" of the country and was careful about projecting a more "humane" image than his father did in order to attract international aid. However, the fiercest Macoutes were not instructed to discontinue their sinister practices, they were simply asked to carry out their tasks away from the glare of publicity. The plan worked: In light of the seeming relaxation of the political climate, the U.S. and other foreign governments promised more aid to Haiti and foreign investors established factories in Port-au-Prince, profiting immensely from the country's cheap labor. In return, some thousands of low wage jobs were created. An atmosphere of economic liberalism emerged: Roads connecting major towns to the capital were rebuilt with the aid of foreign governments, and the telephone system was restored. In addition, the tourist industry was revamped. It is reported that in 1973, 200,000 tourists visited Haiti. As foreign monies poured into the country, the corruption of those in power reached greater heights. In 1975 alone, the World Bank reported that there were some 45 million dollars unaccounted for. As Baby Doc and his cronies enriched themselves and enjoyed all the luxuries of modern life (private ranches, satellite dishes, yachts, fleets of sport cars, and even villas overseas), the majority of the Haitians, particularly those living in rural Haiti, slipped deeper into poverty. As one scholar reports, "the percentage of the population living in extreme poverty rose from 48 per cent in 1976 to 81 per cent in 1985. Under the Duvaliers, Haiti became one of the poorest and most economically polarised countries of the world."[13] Jean-Claude's so-called economic revolution benefited only the local bourgeoisie and business-people. The light assembly industries located in Port-au-Prince and its outskirts were not doing much for the mass of the population living in the countryside. In fact, the gap between the urban and rural areas widened. An exodus from the countryside to Port-au-Prince started as more peasants, who could no longer make a living from eroded small parcels of land, surged into the capital in search of factory jobs. Soon more shantytowns began to mushroom all throughout the city, highlighting the gulf between the haves and the have-nots. In the face of absolute misery, complete neglect, and even persecution by Baby Doc's government, increasing numbers of poor Haitians decided to take their chances and embark on a risky journey across the straits of Florida. Thus, as early as 1972, the phenomenon of the Haitian boat people started, with no end in sight. Between 1980 and 1981, 40,000 boat people made it to the shores of South Florida, and it is estimated that there were already an approximate illegal population of 50,000 between 1972 and 1981. The reception of the Haitian boat people in the United States will be discussed later.

Moreover, Jean-Claude was very sympathetic to the Mulatto merchants and technocrats and began to seek allies among members of this class, thus alienating the old guard upon which his father's power rested. The alliance between the Mulatto and the new regime was sealed in May of 1980, when Jean-Claude Duvalier married the *mulâtresse* Michèle Bennett, daughter of a wealthy speculator. The young head of state and his greedy wife did not mind spending $5 million on their wedding, at a time when the country was depending on foreign aid for its survival and when the majority of the population was living in abject poverty. Further, the insensitivity to the plight of the peasants reached its climax in the early/mid-1980s, when more than a million local pigs were slaughtered, supposedly to prevent African Swine Fever from reaching the North American mainland. By an agreement with the Inter-American Institute of Cooperative Agriculture, the Haitian pigs were to be replaced by "foreign pigs," called *cochons grimèl* (light-skinned pigs) by the Haitian peasants. They were extremely unhappy with this situation, as the care of these *cochons grimèl*—requiring expensive feed and cement pigpens, unlike the Haitian stock—was too costly for them. Eventually, the alienation of the masses would constitute a real menace to the stability of Jean-Claude's government. Unable to make a living and being forced to kill their animals, more peasants continued their rapid and steady exodus to the U.S. shores. The Haitian boat people were, indeed, getting so numerous that they were causing an embarrassment for Baby Doc's regime, at the displeasure of the U.S. government. Anti-Haitian sentiments with regard to the arrival of the boat people were emerging in Florida, and the story of these unfortunate Haitians caught fire. Haitians were portrayed as AIDS carriers and savages, who practiced a mysterious religion called Vodou that involved the drinking of blood from freshly slaughtered animals. As a result of this negative publicity, tourist travel to Haiti plummeted. In 1982–1983, the total number of visitors to Haiti was 10,000, compared with 200,000 in earlier years. American (and other foreign) capitalists started to withdraw their investments, as it was becoming increasingly clear that extreme political and economic instability would prevail in the days to come.

Shunned again by the Americans, and perhaps in hopes of restoring the country's image to the world, the Duvaliers convinced Pope John Paul II to include Haiti on his 1983 March tour of Latin America. The pontiff spoke forcefully about the need for social reform and argued vehemently that "things must change." His holy words became the slogan of the masses; the Liberation Theology emerging in Latin America began to resonate with young Haitian priests who were forming a movement known as *Ti Legliz* (small churches) to advance the cause of social justice and human rights. These *Ti Legliz* were very militant and they spoke against the Macoute bishops and other Macoute priests; consequently, they became very instrumental in organizing grassroots efforts that would destabilize the oppressive Duvalier regime. Father Jean-Bertand Aristide was one of these young *Ti Legliz* priests. In 1985, he was assigned to the Parish of St. Jean Bosco, located in one of the poorest neighborhoods of Port-au-Prince. There, he did not mince his words to call for an end to misery and hunger. Throughout the country, riots were erupting: "Down with Misery and Hunger," and "Things Must Change" were their rallying cries, as angry mobs looted Macoutes' properties and burned government buildings. Armed with machetes, peasants took to the streets chanting, "Down with Duvalier." By early 1986, it had become obvious that the country was in a state of civil war. The army, already discontented with the loss of some of its power to the Garde Présidentielle and the Tontons Macoutes, under the leadership of General Henry Namphy decided to actively intervene to disarm the Macoutes. Jean-Claude Duvalier's days as president-for-life were numbered. The United States agreed to send a U.S. Air Force aircraft to take the first family and its close entourage to France.

The Duvalier era, written in blood, had come to an abrupt end. A military junta known as the *Conseil National de Gouvernement* (CNG) took control of the government. This CNG, led by General Namphy, was mostly composed of military men (five of them). Out of the two civilian members, one had served the Duvaliers for more than twenty years. The charge of the CNG was to set up a democratic election process right away.

THE POST-DUVALIER ERA

The chaotic events of the post-Duvalier era made headline news around the world, and here in the United States CNN viewers might have followed some of the somber news from Haiti. The most salient happenings of this period are highlighted. More bloodshed came in the aftermath of Jean-Claude's departure. The so-called liberated masses began the process of cleansing the country of all the Macoutes they could get their hands and machetes on. This cleansing operation became known as "operation *dechoukaj*" (uprooting operation). By all means, the Macoutes had to be uprooted. It seemed that the country was back to the days of Dessalines, *koupe tèt, boule kay* (cut off heads, and burn houses). Needless to say, in this volatile climate of *dechoukaj,* the country sank into deeper destruction, and during this period foreign aid stopped. In the mist of such carnage, the army, which had always had friends among the Tontons Macoutes, began protecting them and turned its back on the people. Subsequently, confrontations between the army and the masses ensued. The massacre of peasant activists in the northwestern town of Jean Rabel in July of 1987 confirmed the suspicions that there were still a great many Macoutes remaining, and that the army was behind them. Political chaos and mistrust were the order of the day; the Conseil National de Gouvernement, now under intense scrutiny, was not eager to set up a civilian apparatus *(conseil électoral provisoire)* to conduct democratic elections for a new president. Between February 1986 and February 1988, three national governing councils succeeded one another. In November of 1987, elections were finally organized by the *conseil électoral provisoire* for a new president to be sworn in on February 7, 1988. These elections resulted in violence, as convoys of army troops cruised the streets and stormed into voting polls, killing at random voters waiting in line. It was rumored that the "wrong" candidate was ahead. After the aborted November 29, 1987, election, a bogus election, organized this time by the army on January 17, 1988 (with little voter turnout), brought Leslie Manigat, a professor, to the presidency. Manigat did not last; a military coup brought him down on June 20, 1988. General Henry Namphy, who led all three CNGs, assumed power only to find himself *déchouké* three months later by another military coup on September 17, 1988. While power was in the hands of the army, grassroot movements were severely repressed, and the *Ti Legliz* were constantly under attack. The most ferocious of these attacks took place on September 11, 1988, when Father Aristide's St. Jean Bosco parish was burned and scores of parishioners, who were attracted to his message of putting an end to misery and hunger, were slaughtered. The young priest miraculously escaped. However, he fell into complete disgrace with the Salesian order of the Church, which apparently was getting fed up with his brand of radicalism. He was accused by his superiors of encouraging violence and class divisions; eventually he was expelled from the Church in December of 1988. He devoted his energies to an orphanage for street kids and pondered his future as events unfolded. Military terror reigned until March 1990, when Supreme Court Justice Ertha Pascal Trouillot (the first Haitian woman president) was sworn in as interim president. In October of that year, Jean-Bertand Aristide made a shocking announcement: he was entering the presidential race and running under the banner of the *Lavalas* movement (the Creole word for torrential rains that sweep away everything). His movement included peasant and human rights organizations as well as labor unions. Elections were set for December 16, 1990. Under the watchful eyes of a heavy foreign delegation—composed of U.N. and OAS (Organization of American States) observers and of other dignitaries (including former president Jimmy Carter)—the vote was counted: Jean-Bertrand Aristide was the winner, obtaining 67 percent of the vote. On February 7, 1991, the former *Ti Legliz* priest was inaugurated.

Aristide right away made some changes in the army; one that would later prove deadly was the appointment of General Raoul Cédras, as army chief of staff, and subsequently as head of the armed forces. The old Macoutes, as well as their allies in the army, were edgy and not sure of what the new president meant by urging followers to be "vigilant without vengeance." They saw in his rhetoric a "tacit encouragement against further mass actions against [them]."[14] Something had to be done about this clear and present danger. On September 29, 1991 (just seven months after he took office), the army, led by General Cédras, led a coup that sent him in exile in the United States. It is said that his life was spared thanks to the intervention of the French ambassador. Reprisals against Aristide's supporters followed; the masses lost all hope; repression was horrific; more people fled. In the United States, the boat people situation intensified. CNN reported that shortly after the coup, 67,000 illegal Haitians were intercepted and returned to Haiti.[15]

The U.S. government placed an embargo on Haiti. The poorest sectors of the population felt the effects of this embargo, as transportation fares soared with the high cost of gasoline and as other imported goods became in short supply. In the meantime, contraband developed; the local bourgeoisie and some officers in the army who had the monopoly of the contraband traffic enriched themselves. Fearing that more bad times were forthcoming, everyday folks pooled their meager resources together to finance their voyage overseas *(à l'étranger)*, while the poorest of the poor embarked on rickety boats to be picked up by the U.S. Coast Guard. Liberal sectors of the American population, including African American political leaders, were appalled by President George Bush's decision to expatriate Haitian refugees. In this context of protestations, it is worth mentioning an event that received extensive media coverage: In February 1992, renowned African American dancer and anthropologist Katherine Dunham, who lived in Haiti for significant periods of time, began at the age of 82 a 47-day fast at her East St. Louis home, to protest the U.S. deportations of Haitian boat refugees. Dunham agreed to end her fast only at the urging of exiled President Aristide, who visited her personally. In November 1992, the American people put the democratic candidate Bill Clinton in the White House. With help from the U.N., some agreement was put together in an attempt to solve the Haitian impasse. This deal became known as the Governors Island Accord. According to this accord, Aristide was to return to Haiti on October 30, 1993, accompanied by a U.N. peacekeeping force. Opposition to Aristide's return mounted in Haiti, and a group of younger Macoutes (who called themselves FRAPH, Front for the Advancement of Progress in Haiti), were organizing themselves by the force of arms to prevent Aristide and his international force from landing in Haiti. More bloodshed was on the horizon. The Clinton administration was apprised of the situation. The disaster of Mogadishu, Somalia (well depicted in the movie *Black Hawk Down*), in early October provided additional reason not to go forward at that time with the return of Aristide under the terms of the Governors Island Accord. Claiming victory, the army and FRAPH continued their violent deeds and turned up the heat. More people were killed, and reports of rape as a means of repression surfaced. Washington was under pressure to stop vacillating and to take more decisive actions; in July of 1994 a resolution authorizing a direct, U.S. military intervention in Haiti was passed. Troops began training for deployment; navy ships were ordered to head toward Haiti. The U.S. occupation was scheduled to begin on September 19. In this warlike situation, former president Jimmy Carter, accompanied by Senator Sam Nunn and former Joint Chiefs of Staff chairman Colin Powell, went to Haiti the preceding day to persuade General Cédras and his military junta to relinquish power, so that Aristide could return without bloodshed. At the eleventh hour (U.S. military aircraft were already airborne), Cédras accepted Carter's proposal that allowed him to stay in command until October 15, and to accept the intervention of U.S. troops to restore peace and order. As per this arrangement, the United States made its "permissive entry" by landing at the airport on September 19, 1994. Twenty thousand U.S. troops took over.

As agreed, Cédras left in October and went to Panama. On October 15, President Aristide, under the protection of the U.S. military and a delegation of dignitaries (including Reverend Jesse Jackson), returned to Haiti to finish his term, which was to expire on February 7, 1996—in spite of protestations from Aristide's supporters that his term had to be expanded by the three "stolen" years he had spent in exile. It is said that Aristide reluctantly relinquished power to his prime minister, René Préval, after the elections held on December 17, 1995. Further, it was rumored that Préval was not really in charge and that Aristide was the one governing the country behind the scenes, diligently campaigning for reelection when Préval would finish his term in February 2001. Some saw in his behavior a tendency toward a *dérive totalitaire* (totalitarian drift).[16] Subsequently, Aristide won the new presidential elections (tainted by alleged fraud), and he was slated to serve a second term as president until February 2006. However, Aristide's second term in office was fraught with turmoil, resentment, discontent, and strong allegations of corruption and violence. He met with ferocious opposition from various sectors of society, which culminated in another coup that forced him to leave the country on February 29, 2004.

Aristide, upon his return in 1994, was specifically instructed by Washington and the international financial institutions to tone down his brand of rhetoric, filled with anticapitalist fervor, and to put the country on a path to "reconciliation." This was the sine qua non condition to regain foreign aid. He was forced to consider, as one scholar puts it, "a more conservative structural adjustment program under U.S. tutelage."[17] This structural adjustment program (SAP), mandated primarily by the United States, entailed, among other things, the privatization of state-owned enterprises. It was not obvious where the masses fit in this scenario that links foreign financial monopolies with Haitian businesspeople (i.e., the Haitian bourgeoisie). Aristide was hesitant to challenge the roots of dominant class power; consequently, signs of discontent and disenchantment began to surface in the *Lavalas* movement itself. It was alleged that he turned his back on his own kind. Internal power struggles began to erupt, thus eroding Aristide's support base. Opposition was growing, crystallized in the formation of an alternative movement called *Convergence Démocratique*. This opposition group was said to be composed of former allies of Aristide, old duvalierists, and reactionary bourgeois, and it regrouped 15 political parties. Aristide's supporters responded to opposition by forming their own bands, known as *Chimères,* who were said to engage in criminal activities and a great deal of violence. Indeed, it was impossible, based on reports from Haiti (well publicized in the U.S. media as well the Haitian diasporic media), to assert that things were going well and that the country was on a path to recovery. In fact, on December 17, 2001, a coup d'état was attempted to overthrow Aristide. Although the disgruntled members of the disbanded army to whom the coup is attributed did not succeed then, their actions went a long way in demonstrating the state of chaos and confusion that prevailed in Haiti under Aristide's administration. As one scholar, who has looked closely at the Haitian situation from 1994 to 2002, warns, "at the moment, the country suffers from a general and profound malaise that can easily turn into a fundamental systematic crisis with unpredictable consequences."[18]

How prophetic were his words! Indeed, the climate of profound malaise intensified during the period from September 2003 to February 2004, a period that witnessed tensions between university students and police, and clashes between Aristide's supporters and opponents during which many people were killed. In early February 2004, anti-government militants, known as the rebels, seized Gonaïves, Haiti's fourth largest city. These rebels were led by Louis Jodel Chamblain, a convicted former leader of the group called FRAPH that in the early 1990s opposed Aristide, and by Guy Philippe, a former member of the disbanded army and former police chief. The uprising soon spread to at least nine other towns; on February 22, the northern city of Cap-Haitian fell to the rebels who vowed to attack the capital of Port-au-Prince in their campaign to oust Aristide. A U.S.-led diplomatic mission presented Haiti's government and opposition with a peace plan that was rejected by the opposition. Pressure continued to mount for Aristide to step down, as the violence could not be controlled and chaos reigned in the capital. It is alleged that the U.S. government told Aristide that arrangements could be made to ensure his safety if he chose to leave the country. On Sunday, February 29, 2004, President Aristide left Haiti, amid conflicting reports of the exact circumstances surrounding his departure. It was reported in the media that an unmarked white jet took off from Port-au-Prince carrying Aristide and his wife; twenty hours later, the plane landed in the Central African Republic. A few hours later, Supreme Court Justice Boniface Alexandre became Aristide's constitutional successor. Gérard Latortue, who spent most of his career abroad with the United Nations Industrial Development Organization, was chosen by a council of sages *(conseil des sages)* to be prime minister. A post-Aristide era filled with uncertainties had begun.

In light of this climate, Haitian immigration (legal or illegal) to the United States might not abate in any foreseeable future. In fact, an article published in the *Haitian Times* (June 11–17, 2003, issue) already warned that Haitian professionals are also fleeing Haiti, since "as they looked to the future," all they see is "high unemployment, political instability, insecurity." Many rely on family in the United States to "send for them."

CULTURAL LEGACY

Scholars describe Haiti as a country of "political failures" but "cultural successes," and acknowledge that "an original and vibrant culture has thrived for nearly two centuries in spite of politics."[19] Like migration patterns, it is also through the study of history that Haitian cultural identity can be explained. The richness and breadth of Haitian culture that emerged in the early days of independence continues to flourish to the present day and is visible in Haitian diasporic communities in the United States. Some of its core elements include a strong sense of racial pride, deeply rooted religious beliefs and practices, the value attached to landholding no matter how small the property, and a real enthusiasm for artistic and literary creativity. Racial pride is perhaps the stronger equalizer of class and color distinction in Haiti, as it is a marker of solidarity among all Haitians and it is also the strongest cultural legacy of independence.

The greatest significance of Haiti's independence is that by overturning a White government, it "presented a radical challenge to colonialism, to slavery and to the associated ideology of White radicalism."[20] Independent Haiti became the symbol of African regeneration, Black power, Black freedom, and racial equality. The success of Haiti provided "a gleam of hope" for the rest of the Black world and provided inspiration to other Caribbean colonies as well as North American Blacks who looked at Haiti as a "sign of redemption" and a "potential centre of Black resistance to colonialism, slavery and oppression."[21] In the words of authoritative African American abolitionist Frederick Douglass, "the mission of Haiti was to give the world a new and true revelation of the black man's character. This mission she has performed and has performed it well."[22] All throughout the nineteenth century, Haitians sought to give hope to the slave population of the New World, and they vehemently deplored the misery and prejudice that afflicted their African brothers still held in bondage in the United States. In fact, the immigration of Blacks from the United States was welcome, as Haiti considered itself the homeland of displaced African people in the New World. African Americans thought of Haiti as the guardian of liberty, and they began to identify with Haitians in their own quest for freedom. In fact, several African Americans started migrating to Haiti during the 1820s and beyond. As one scholar notes, "during the nineteenth century, African American freedmen migrated to Haiti in two emigration waves, one in 1824 and another in 1859," being drawn by the promise of freedom.[23] The same scholar asserts:

> For people of African descent, the Haitian revolution had an even greater significance than either the American or the French Revolution. The American Declaration of Independence proclaimed the equality of all men and outlined their inalienable rights, yet the rights of slaves were conspicuously denied. Subsequently, the French Revolution reaffirmed these rights in the Declaration of the Rights of Man and the Citizen in 1789. Even after this declaration, however, the practice of slavery persisted in the French colonies. The Haitian Revolution fulfilled man's universal aspiration to be free by including people of African descent.[24]

Moreover, the Haitian Revolution was seen as a model for other liberation movements in Latin America. For example, in 1815, Venezuelan revolutionary leaders Francisco Miranda and Simón Bolívar sought President Pétion's help in their efforts to free South America from Spanish control. In return for Pétion's help, Bolívar agreed to free the slaves in Venezuela. Pétion is not only known to Haitians for his role in the independence of the country, he is also recognized as a great liberator by the Spanish American world.

Haiti's successful slave revolution is at the root of Haitians' pride in their race. From the beginning of their national history, Haitians have considered themselves the rightful leaders and spokespersons for all Black people. For Haitians, Black has never meant inferiority or invisibility; it is synonymous with pride and unflinching independence. Their race is the symbol of a glorious past, that of the revolution that led to freedom, to nationhood, and perhaps most important, to equality with Whites. By winning their independence in the early nineteenth century, Haitians have resolved issues of race and national identity conflicts that are still being fought in many Third World countries as well as in the United States. Haitians know that they are a Black people, *not an inferior people*. This perception is a direct legacy of Haitian history, where after independence, the country was racially unified under the

"Black flag," all Whites having been killed or having hastily left in fear for their lives. Haitians have formed a nation-based interpretation of race, according to which Blackness is equated with nationhood. This strong pride in Blackness that Haitians have developed for two centuries causes them to vehemently resent the minority status that is assigned to them when they migrate to the United States, as will be fully discussed in subsequent chapters. Moreover, this same sense of pride, at times, can translate in a feeling of superiority over other Blacks, particularly African Americans, who in spite of the abolition of slavery have not to date escaped White domination.

During the U.S. occupation, Haitians felt they suffered a terrible humiliation. Therefore, it comes as no surprise that an indigenist writing movement began to flourish in the 1920s, characterized by fierce nationalism and anti-U.S. sentiments. In reaction to White occupation, Haitian nationalist intellectuals and writers advanced an ethnological ideology, which became known as *noirisme*. This ideology advocated the fundamental notion that Black people have a personality that is peculiar to them and different from that of the White race. Consequently, writers stressed cultural authenticity and urged Haitians to look for their roots in African traditions and beliefs. The Vodou religion, the Creole language, and aspects of folk culture became celebrated. Ironically enough, young François Duvalier was a strong advocate of this ethnological ideology. One of the chief proponents of the indigenist movement was Jean Price-Mars, who has been considered the father, or the precursor, of the *Négritude* movement that emerged in Paris under the leadership of Senegalese President Léopold Sédar Senghor. Jean Price-Mars's acclaimed work *Ainsi Parla l'Oncle* (*So Spoke the Uncle*, published in 1928) is a classic that has found its way into the canon of Black literature and philosophy. Other Haitian writers, such as Félix Morisseau-Leroy, began writing poetry in Haitian Creole, thus championing the cause of the national language in the literary domain. He is also well-known for his Creole translations of classical French dramas, such as *Antigone*. Another influential writer of that period is undoubtedly Jacques Roumain, the first Haitian writer to achieve international recognition with his novel *Gouverneurs de la rosée (Masters of the Dew)*. This particular novel exemplified the best elements of Haitian indigenism, as it gives particular attention to the peasant class. The significance of this novel can be seen in the fact that it has been translated into more than a dozen languages, and adapted for theater and cinema. Perhaps the best-known English translation of Roumain's novel is that of Langston Hughes and Mercer Cook, former chairperson of the Department of Modern Languages at Atlanta University. Part of Roumain's international appeal resides in the fact that "he associated the interests of the Haitian masses with those of the proletariat in metropolitan countries."[25] Roumain's *Masters of the Dew* is regularly taught in Black literature courses in many U.S. universities. The same indigenist revival is also seen in another literary group that flourished around the same period, the *Griots,* which takes its name from a very well-known African word *griot,* a poet, a storyteller, who perpetuates tribal traditions, customs, and beliefs.

If Haiti was politically and economically shunned by the world powers, it was emerging as a country with a rich literary tradition. Many important Third World writers, including Cuban Alejo Carpentier and Martinican Edouard Glissant and Aimé Césaire, have been inspired by Haitian indigenist writers and Haitian history. Likewise, African American intellectuals, who already considered Haiti "the torchbearer of freedom," also began to recognize it as a "new mecca for black culture," in the context of the rise of Black nationalism in the United States.[26] Consequently, many went to the Caribbean nation to better understand their own Black heritage. Black nationalist Marcus Garvey, founder of the Universal Negro Improvement Association (UNIA), emphasized the relevance of Haiti's historical past because Haiti was the land where the Negroes repelled the Whites and established an independent republic. He further stressed that African Americans should identify with Toussaint Louverture and Dessalines. In the same vein, writers of the Harlem Renaissance embraced Haiti's history and culture. Claude McKay's work, for example, is replete with tales of Haiti's heroic past. Langston Hughes, perhaps the most central figure of the Harlem Renaissance movement, having read of "Toussaint L'Ouverture, Dessalines, King Christophe, proud Black names," made a pilgrimage to Haiti. He went to the city of Cap Haitian, "where the slaves years ago planned the revolt that shook the foundations of human bondage in the Western World."[27] While in Haiti, Hughes met Jacques Roumain, and the two formed a lasting friendship, sharing the same social and political consciousness. Subsequently, Hughes published a historical drama, *Emperor of Haiti* (1939), that focused on the accomplishments of Dessalines. Novelist Zora Neale Hurston also took an interest in Haiti in her search for the Vodou religion and traveled throughout the country for an in-depth discovery of its practices. Similarly, renowned dancer and anthropologist Katherine Dunham—mentioned earlier for her fast of protest against the deportation of the Haitian boat people—also went to Haiti to find the richness of African dances and rituals. She lived there for a significant period of time and it is said that she even became a Vodou priestess. In 1947, she published an acclaimed work, *The Dances of Haiti.* Other well-known African Americans who visited Haiti during the same time period included authoritative scholar and founding member of the NAACP (National Association for the Advancement of Colored People) W. E. B. Du Bois, writer and diplomat James Weldon Johnson, and Howard University philosophy professor Alain Leroy Locke. Other literary dignitaries included French surrealist André Breton and French philosopher Jean-Paul Sartre. Those friendships and literary alliances go a long way in showing the importance of Haitian letters. One scholar observes that "despite this massive impoverished reading public, those who wrote in Haiti have published more books than any other Caribbean country."[28] Haitians are well aware of the privileged place they occupy in literary traditions, and this is a source of great pride for them.

It is also important to note that Haitian writers were attracted to the works of African American writers as well, many of which have been translated into French. For example, Price-Mars himself in his quest for a new Haitian literature deeply rooted in African cultural values took notice of the works of well-known African American intellectuals such as James Weldon Johnson, W. E. B. Du Bois, Booker T. Washington, and Langston Hughes, among others. Further, all throughout the 1930s and 1940s, Haitian intellectuals traveled to the United States and were involved in all sorts of literary and cultural activities in U.S. institutions. For example, renowned Haitian poet Jean Brierre attended Columbia University, and Haitian intellectual and statesman Dantès Bellegarde lectured at Atlanta University in the summers of 1937 and 1940, respectively. Bellegarde also served as Haitian minister in Washington.

The Haitian indigenist movement that flourished during the U.S. occupation of Haiti (1915–1934) coincided with the rise of Black Nationalism in the United States. A few years earlier, in 1909, Black American intellectuals had founded the National Association for the Advancement of Colored People. In their struggle for racial equality, they regarded Haiti as the keeper of liberty in the New World. Consequently, when the U.S. Marines landed in Haiti, strong indignation surfaced within the NAACP. In the *Crisis* (the major publication of the NAACP), W. E. B. Du Bois registered his resentment: "The United States has violated the independence of a sister state. With absolutely no adequate excuse she made a white American Admiral sole and irresponsible dictator of Hayti."[29] In addition, he used this journal to garner African American opposition to the occupation. More important though, African American leaders feared that Haiti might lose its independence. Throughout the occupation period, the NAACP sought to denounce the negative effects of the American intervention on the Haitian people, and the devastating consequences of this so-called dollar diplomacy. James Weldon Johnson, who headed the NAACP during part of this period, spent three months in Haiti and met with important Haitian intellectuals, among them Price-Mars, Roumain, and Bellegarde. W. E. B. Du Bois also befriended these

Haitian scholars. Not surprisingly, the U.S. occupation brought Haitian and African American intellectuals together and solidified the ties between these two groups. The fall of Haiti was thought to be the fall of Black Americans; their interests were bound. In short, the NAACP fought vehemently to end the U.S. occupation of Haiti; it was the leading organization in the United States, that campaigned for the departure of the marines and for the end of the financial control of the U.S. banks in Haiti.

In addition to its literary and intellectual legacy, Haiti is well known throughout the world for its artistic expression. The first art form that developed right after independence was portrait and historical painting. In December of 1980, an exhibition titled "Haitian History as Seen by Its Painters" showcased a great many of these paintings and documented the existence of Haitian art as early as the nineteenth century. However, it was in the 1940s that Haitian art really emerged on the international scene. This recognition is attributed to the American watercolorist Dewitt Peters, who in 1944 went to Haiti as an English teacher and founded the Centre d'Art, "where Haitians would come and paint and exchange ideas without having to follow academic lectures, fostering a state of mind favorable to artistic development."[30] Some artists at the Centre d'Art developed an art form that is called primitive or naive art. It focuses on nature and daily life, and Vodou rhythm and structure. One notes that these themes coincide with those of the indigenist literary movement. Eminent personalities visited the Centre d'Art, including André Breton—who gave special attention to Haitian art in his book *Surrealism and Painting*—Cuban painter Wilfredo Lam, and renowned Cuban art critique José Gomez-Sicré. In 1947, a UNESCO art exhibition held in Paris at the Museum of Modern Art featured the work of the Vodouist painter Hector Hyppolite, thus bringing a great deal of visibility to Haitian artistic traditions. The nationally and internationally known Galerie d'Art Nader, which opened in Port-au-Prince in 1966, has the finest collection of Haitian paintings in Haiti available for purchase, consequently contributing to the dissemination of Haitian art, as it receives hundreds of visitors and customers from around the world. Over the years, the gallery expanded with branches in the Dominican Republic and Florida. Other artists also trained at the Centre d'Art, such as Georges Liautaud, developed an ironwork art form and produced decorative metal sculptures. These structures could represent a variety of things: snakes, dragons, mermaids, and many other creatures. Other artists expressed their talents through the designing of sequined flags that are used in Vodou ceremonies. In fact, in the 1980s and 1990s, sequined flags produced in Haiti, depicting representations of Vodou *lwas* really caught the attention of foreigners. As recently as the mid/late 1990s, the Fowler Museum at the University of California–Los Angeles organized a very successful exhibition entitled "Sacred Arts of Haitian Vodou" that toured a number of major cities, including New York City, where the exhibit was housed at the Museum of Natural History in the fall of 1998.[31] The Milwaukee Art Museum is home to the largest collection of Haitian art in the United States and, in fact, in the world. This collection of Haitian art classics, named the Flagg collection, was originally purchased by the late multimillionaire Richard Flagg (and his wife, Erna) at the urging of his friend, Monsignor Alfred Voegeli, the Episcopalian Bishop of Haiti who was from Milwaukee. Upon his death, the collection was bequeathed to the Milwaukee Art Museum.

Music is certainly another form of artistic expression that has brought a great deal of visibility to Haitians.[32] Haiti has a longstanding musical tradition ranging from folkloric music to Creole rap singers. One popular indigenous form of music that is very popular and is used in Vodou ceremonies is the *Rara*. *Rara* rhythms originated with the peasant class and are embedded with African traditions. *Rara* bands perform in the streets at various times when there are particular political events that incite grassroot movements. However, the established tradition of the *Rara* festival is during the Lent season, right after Carnival up until Easter Sunday. Because *Rara* uses songs that can also be found in the traditional Vodou repertoire, it has attracted the attention of scholars. Elizabeth McAlister, for instance, wrote extensively on the topic in her book *Rara! Vodou, Power, Performance in Haiti and Its Diaspora*. This is how she describes *Rara*:

> Rara is the yearly festival in Haiti that even more than Carnival, belongs to the so-called peasant class and the urban poor. Beginning the moment Carnival ends, on the eve of Lent, and building for six weeks until Easter Week, Rara processions walk for miles through local territory, attracting fans and singing new and old songs. Bands stop traffic for hours to play music and perform rituals for Afro-Haitian deities at crossroads, bridges, and cemeteries. They are conducting the spiritual work that is necessary when the angels and saints, along with Jesus, disappear in the underworld on Good Friday.[33]

In the mid-1950s, another well known form of music in Haiti known as *Compas* (or *Konpa* in Creole) developed, based on the influence of the *Meringue* from the Dominican Republic. For many years, *Konpa* dominated the Haitian musical scene with such artists as Weber Sicot and Nemours Jean-Baptiste. As one scholar notes, "*Compas* marks the emergence of a music industry in Haiti and is the first Haitian popular music to achieve commercial success."[34] In the late 1960s and early 1970s, with the international rise of rock music, young Haitian musicians, some from the middle class, began to produce their own version of *Konpa* music and formed other types of music known as *Combo*. These groups began using *conga* drums in their music, and soon musical ensembles called *mini jazz* proliferated all over the country. Tabou Combo—which was formed in Haiti and relocated to New York when the political situation worsened in the late 1970s—and Miami-based T-Vice are two bands illustrative of this type of music. The deterioration of the country forced many musicians to leave Haiti, taking their art with them to New York and Miami. Consequently, new musical interests developed that sought to return to Haitian folk forms, in particular Vodou and *Rara* musical traditions. These new interests crystallized in 1978 with the formation of a group called Boukman Eksperyans. This group takes its name after the famous slave Boukman, who presided over the ceremony of the Bois-Caïman on the night of August 14, 1791, held to set the final details of the massive slave insurrection that would eventually lead to Saint-Domingue's independence (as can be recalled from chapter 2). This newer form of music is known as *mizik rasin,* meaning "roots music." Through their music and lyrics, artists spoke against the abuses of the Duvalier regime, and allied themselves with the struggle of the masses. This explains the strong use of *Rara* traditions in their music. In 1990, Boukman Ekperyans won the Carnival Song prize in Haiti, with its popular song *Kè m pap sote* (My heart will not leap). According to Haitians' anecdotes, this revolutionary song may have paved the way for Aristide's presidential election victory in 1991. Moreover, Boukman Eksperyans achieved international acclaim with the release of its album *Vodou Adjae,* nominated for a Grammy Award. As one scholar observes, *mizik rasin* appeals to "grassroots movement against dictatorship and the mobilization of the previously marginalized peasant majority, [and it] quickly captured the mood of the nation with lyrics that both criticized the military and praised Haitian peasant culture and beliefs."[35] In short, Haitians have good reason to be proud of their artistic achievements, and the visibility that Haitian literature, art, and music have gained might palliate some of the negative portrayals of Haitians in the media.

This chapter has provided a description of the historical backdrop against which Haitian immigration to the United States must be understood. It has shown the interconnectedness of the economic and political situation. For this reason, it can be asserted that a great number of Haitians are migrating to escape political hardships. However, in spite of an endless cycle of political failures, this chapter has also highlighted the rich cultural traditions that Haitians bring with them to the United States. These traditions are perhaps the greatest legacy of Haitian immigration to this country and are well interwoven with its contemporary cultural fabric.

Popular Haitian band Boukman Eksperyans. Courtesy of the *Haitian Times*.

Haitian American performer rocks the fans at the 2003 Flag Day Celebration. Courtesy of the *Haitian Times*.

NOTES

1. Heinl, Heinl, and Heinl (1995: 172).
2. Dash (2001: 11).
3. Heinl, Heinl, and Heinl (1995: 147).
4. Arthur and Dash (1999: 209).
5. Nicholls (1996: 144–46); see also Plummer (1992: chap. 5).
6. Nicholls (1996: 148).
7. Ibid.
8. Suzy Castor (1988), as quoted in Arthur and Dash (1999: 223).
9. Plummer (1992: 102).
10. Dash (2001: 16).
11. Ibid., p. 17.
12. Heinl, Heinl, and Heinl (1995: 612).
13. Arthur and Dash (1999: 49).
14. Heinl, Heinl, and Heinl (1995: 734).
15. CNN, October 30, 2002, report posted on the Web at: http://www.cnn.com/2002/US/South/10/30/haitians.ashore/index.html.
16. Fatton (2002: 112).
17. Ibid., p. 108.
18. Ibid., p. 110.
19. Weistein and Segal (1984: 156–57).
20. Nicholls (1996: 3).
21. Ibid., p. 4.
22. As quoted in Pamphile (2001: 8).
23. Pamphile (2001: 174).
24. Ibid., p. 10.
25. Nicholls (1996: 173).
26. Pamphile (2001: 129).
27. As quoted in Pamphile (2001: 133).
28. Dash (2001: 95).
29. As quoted in Pamphile (2001: 102).
30. Dewitt Peters (1980), as quoted in Gérald Alexis (2000: 10). Alexis's work, *Peintres Haïtiens* (there is an English version), is a very good sourcebook on Haitian art, containing a magnificent display of photographs.
31. See also Donald Cosentino's work *Sacred Heart of Haitian Vodou* (1995). This work also contains beautiful pictures.
32. One of the most authoritative works on Haitian music is Averill (1997).
33. McAlister (2002: 3).
34. Dash (2001: 129).
35. Arthur (2002: 79).

4

Coming to the United States

HAITIAN IMMIGRATION PATTERNS TO THE UNITED STATES

Haitian immigration to the United States must be understood in light of the various events that have taken place throughout Haiti's history. Haitians have come to the United States because they feel compelled to leave their country as they have no other way to survive. As was underscored in the historical sketch, periods of intense political and economic turmoil correlate highly with intense Haitian migration to the United States. The first recorded wave of Haitians, comprising mostly Black intellectuals, occurred during the troublesome period of the U.S. occupation during the 1920s and early 1930s. Duvalier's ascension to the political scene and all the atrocities committed under his regime resulted in accelerated migration from 1960 through the early 1970s. The yearly numbers for that period, as listed in the *Statistical Yearbooks* of the Immigration and Naturalization Service, are presented in table 4.1.

THE PAPA DOC YEARS

In addition to these immigrant figures, the nonimmigrant admission numbers reveal the same increasing patterns of migration. The nonimmigrant category (tourists, students, transit aliens, temporary workers, and trainees) provides the largest number of illegal aliens (see table 4.2). There is little doubt that the regime of terror that allowed Papa Doc to maintain his power

Table 4.1
Legal Immigration Patterns of Haitians (1960–1971)

Year	Number of Immigrants
1960	931
1961	1,025
1962	1,322
1963	1,850
1964	2,082
1965	3,609
1966	3,801
1967	3,567
1968	6,806
1969	6,542
1970	6,932
1971	7,444

Table 4.2
Haitian Nonimmigrants Admitted on Temporary Visas (1960–1971)

Year	Number of Nonimmigrants
1960	4,107
1961	3,822
1962	4,694
1963	4,650
1964	6,341
1965	8,090
1966	9,271
1967	10,880
1968	17,259
1969	19,209
1970	24,535
1971	25,299

caused massive numbers of Haitians to lose all hopes for a decent life in Haiti. François Duvalier's true legacy is the social and economic ruin of Haiti. One scholar asserts that "between 30,000 and 60,000 people were killed by state terrorism" during his 14-year reign. The same scholar goes on to say that foreign aid during the Papa Doc years "had been squandered and pilfered at the approximate rate of 80 per cent," thus depleting the treasury "of some $10 million per year."[1] Moreover, the designation of his son as his successor sent a chilling message to ordinary citizens that duvalierism was not about to disappear with his death. Consequently, more desperate Haitians found ways to leave their country and to seek new lives in the United States. This sign of despair is well reflected in the immigration patterns that accelerated as Haitians moved deeper and deeper into the somber years of absolute dictatorship.

THE BABY DOC YEARS

In a similar manner, immigration during Baby Doc's administration intensified. As was explained, the political and economic situation of the country worsened as the corruption of those in power knew no limits. For the deprived masses living in extreme poverty in the rural areas, the so-called economic revolution was devoid of any meaning whatsoever. Out of their desperation, the Haitian boat people phenomenon was born (see tables 4.3 and 4.4). The INS indicates that there are gaps in the historical nonimmigrant data. These gaps occurred between 1980 and 1982. Ironically, these gap periods seem to have occurred when the highest estimates of boat people have been suggested by scholars and chroniclers, who themselves had relied on eyewitness accounts to reconstruct those migratory events.

Table 4.3
Legal Immigration Patterns of Haitians (1972–1986)

Year	Number of Immigrants
1972	5,809
1973	4,786
1974	3,946
1975	5,146
1976	6,691
1977	5,441
1978	6,470
1979	6,433
1980	6,540
1981	6,683
1982	8,779
1983	8,424
1984	9,839
1985	10,165
1986	12,666

Table 4.4
Haitian Nonimmigrants Admitted on Temporary Visas (1972–1986)

Year	Number of Nonimmigrants
1972	28,351
1973	32,523
1974	37,287
1975	42,589
1976	70,934
1977	52,091
1978	33,000
1979	79,000
1980	-------
1981	-------
1982	-------
1983	-------
1984	75,000
1985	87,698
1986	86,330

Therefore, in addition to these figures recorded by the INS, one must not forget to include unrecorded numbers of boat people, some of whom had successfully managed to reach the Florida shores unapprehended by the U.S. authorities. As was stated earlier, the Haitian boat people began in 1972. In August of 1978, Congressman Joshua Eilberg of Pennsylvania estimated their number at 8,000.[2] Their boats left from the coasts of Port-de-Paix, Cap-Haitian, and Jérémie, and could carry as many as 100 people on each crossing. For the year 1981, "it was estimated that there were at least 50 or 60 such boats operating from the north coast, together capable of transporting approximately 6,000 Haitians per month."[3] Another report from the U.S. General Accounting Office released in 1982 states that the Immigration and Naturalization Service "had apprehended 47,666 Haitians entering or attempting to enter Florida without authorization since the early 1970's."[4]

THE POST-DUVALIER YEARS

The overthrow of Jean-Claude Duvalier led to more political chaos, as opposition grew between the masses seeking to exterminate all Macoutes and former duvalierists with their operation *dechoukaj* and the army that put in place three successive military governing councils from 1986 through 1988. As explained in chapter 3, in this three-year period the hope for democracy was dissipated with the massacre of peasant activists (July 1987), and of hundreds of voters waiting to cast their ballots at the voting polls (November 1988). Both the immigrant and nonimmigrant numbers that the INS placed at 34,806 and 94,819, respectively, for 1988 capture poignantly the devastation that resulted from those events. Another catastrophic year was 1991, when democratically elected President Aristide was overthrown by a military coup. Many of his supporters, fearing for their lives, fled hastily. Once again, the INS figures for 1991 reflect the political mood of Haiti: 47,527 Haitians were admitted as immigrants and another 73,994 as nonimmigrants. In addition to these figures, let us remember a CNN report indicating that 67,000 boat people were intercepted during the same year. Further, the presidency of Aristide was fraught with controversy and gave rise to more political chaos and violence. Remember the discussion about the *Chimères* (Aristide's bands of supporters) and the opposition movement regrouped under the label *Convergence Démocratique* presented in chapter 3. It is, therefore, not surprising to see Haiti's current political climate of instability well reflected in the influx of Haitians who entered the United States between 1996 and 2000.[5] After a slight drop between 1992 and 1995, the numbers steadily started climbing again. Moreover, the apprehension of the latest wave of boat people in South Florida, as recently as October 2002, attests convincingly to the insecurity that still plagues Haiti, as this is written. In short, the Haitian immigration patterns to the United States speak for themselves: they persuasively tell the grim story of a people trapped in a never-ending political and economic nightmare (see tables 4.5 and 4.6).

HAITIAN SETTLEMENTS IN THE UNITED STATES

The U.S. 2000 census places the number of Haitian immigrants in the United States at 385,000; this number represents a 37 percent increase from the 280,874 immigrants indicated in the 1990 census. However, there is good reason to suggest that this official number is lower than the reality. An article published in the *Haitian Times* (November 27–December 3, 2002), "Census Bureau Lowballs Haitian Count, Experts Say," contends that the figures

Table 4.5
Legal Immigration Patterns of Haitians (1987–2000)

Year	Number of Immigrants
1987	14,819
1988	34,806
1989	13,658
1990	20,324
1991	47,527
1992	11,002
1993	10,094
1994	13,333
1995	14,021
1996	18,386
1997	15,057
1998	13,449
1999	16,532
2000	22,364

reported by the Census Bureau "fall short of population estimates." It goes on to report that several analysts from the Miami-Dade County Department of Planning and Zoning, the New York City Population Division, and the Census Bureau itself admit that these numbers are "low." These analysts attribute the undercount for the Haitian community "to language barriers, address changes, and ancestry questions." They believe that "examples [of ancestry] might not be clear enough to help people decide where they belong."[6] In addition to these explanations, one needs to bear in mind that a significant number of Haitians simply do not fill out census forms for two fundamental reasons: First, illegal immigrants (perhaps as much as one-half of the population) have no intentions of recording their presence with U.S. officials for fear of deportation. Second, even among the legal population, a relatively large segment does not want to be bothered with forms that it does not consider user-friendly, and that it cannot read or properly understand. Moreover, when one looks at other estimates given by other sources (INS, newspapers,

Table 4.6
Haitian Nonimmigrants Admitted on Temporary Visas (1987–2000)

Year	Number of Nonimmigrants
1987	87,392
1988	94,819
1989	93,181
1990	83,227
1991	73,994
1992	52,801
1993	49,510
1994	41,477
1995	62,269
1996	61,397
1997	--------
1998	70,287
1999	85,224
2000	86,494

Note: INS states that "no reliable [nonimmigrant] data are available for 1997."

state publications, among others), the number of Haitian immigrants increases. For these reasons, one can reasonably assert that the total number of Haitians currently residing in the United States (legal and illegal) is in reality much closer to one million.

Haitian immigrants came at various times starting in the late 1920s through the present day. The earlier waves of Haitians, from the time of the U.S. occupation through the Duvalier era, settled primarily in New York City. These patterns are documented by the records of the New York City Department of City Planning, which indicate that 76.1 percent of the Haitian population settled in the Big Apple during the period from 1965 to 1969; 69 percent from 1970 to 1974; 63.6 percent from 1975 to 1980; and 52.2 percent from 1980 to 1985.[7] The first waves of these immigrants were to a great extent composed of middle-class Haitians who came from urban Haiti. Moreover, fieldwork conducted both in Boston and Chicago attested to the existence of a relatively small middle-class Haitian enclave that established its residence also in these two metropolitan areas in the late 1950s and early 1960s. However, in more recent years from the mid-1980s to the present, the state of Florida (the cities of Miami, Fort Lauderdale and West Palm Beach, in particular) has been receiving the largest numbers of the new arrivals. In fact, an article, published in the *Miami Herald* (August 7, 2001), talks about a "quantum leap" in the Haitian population currently residing in the state of Florida. Based on information released by the U.S. Census Bureau, the article states that between 1990 and 2000 the Haitian population "more than doubled to 267,689," and this group leads the Caribbean population of the state. The same article places the Haitian population in the state of New York at 180,000. Moreover, if we look at the INS figures for the period 1987 through 2000, this is what we find for New York City (NYC), Miami, Fort Lauderdale (FL), and West Palm Beach (WPB), respectively (see Table 4.7). The bulk of the remaining population is concentrated in the northeast cities of Boston and Newark (New Jersey). A joint publication released by the Massachusetts Office of Refugee and Immigrant Health, the Bureau of Family and Community Health, and the Department of Public Health (May 1998) lists the Haitian population in Boston at 40,000/45,000; and that of the state at 70,000/75,000.[8] Another estimate released by the Boston Redevelopment Authority places the number of Haitians living in Boston at 46,200 and lists Haiti as its top immigrant country (November 1999).[9] The same *Haitian Times* Census article (mentioned at the beginning of this section) puts the population of Haitians living in New Jersey at 39,902; most of these Haitians are found in the city of Newark. The city of Chicago—representing the Midwest region—has the smallest Haitian population (legal and illegal) of the metropolitan areas mentioned. Nonetheless, it has a sizeable community, of which several members established their residency there some thirty years ago. Information obtained for the state of Illinois and the city of Chicago is not as clear: estimates range from 15,000 to 30,000 for the state and from 5,000 to 15,000 for the Windy City. However, INS records for 1985 through 2000 put the Haitian population in Chicago at closer to 2,000. By adding the figures for earlier years and factoring in the illegal immigrants, there might be good reason to infer that the Haitian population in Chicago falls somewhere between 5,000 and 10,000.

To summarize, if we consider states, Florida with 267,689 Haitian immigrants now appears to have the largest number of the legal and illegal population as it is the destination of the desperate boat people; New York State follows with 180,000. If we consider metropolitan areas, New York City still has the largest concentration, and it reflects a greater diversity within the pop-

Table 4.7
Residential Distribution of Haitians in Selected Cities (1987–2000)

Year	US	NYC	Miami	FL	WPB
1987	14,819	6,274	3,533	444	297
1988	34,806	6,075	13,367	2,882	3,570
1989	13,658	6,141	1,861	570	395
1990	20,324	8,056	3,635	1,326	1,002
1991	47,527	8,141	15, 996	4,919	6,180
1992	11,002	2,288	3,536	1,573	733
1993	10,094	3,325	1,925	740	577
1994	13,333	4,085	2,294	1,144	903
1995	14,021	3,040	2,329	1,274	1,111
1996	18,386	3,896	3,139	1,659	1,611
1997	15,057	3,475	3,048	1,476	1,566
1998	13,449	2,769	2,799	1496	1335
1999	16,532	3,877	2,929	1,535	1,513
2000	22,364	4,351	3,953	2,550	2,416

ulation itself. For additional accuracy, the numbers given by the INS for the immigrant population of New York City and Miami for the period 1985–2000 were tallied, and here are the results: 79,113 people were admitted legally to New York City and indicated the Big Apple as their "metropolitan statistical area of intended residence," and 67,010 for the Miami metropolitan statistical area. When we factor in the earlier numbers (from mid-1960s to 1984), this brings the New York City metropolitan area's legal population at roughly 156,000, and that of Miami-Dade County at approximately 100,000. These INS figures are very close to those mentioned in the aforementioned *Haitian Times* article: Haitians living in South Florida comprise 95,669 in Miami-Dade County and 62,342 in Broward County (which includes Fort Lauderdale); Haitians in the New York metropolitan area comprise 118,769 in the city of New York proper and another 41,550 in the combined counties of Westchester, Nassau, Suffolk, and Rockland (all parts of the greater New York metropolitan statistical area). Within these counties, the towns of Spring Valley (Rockland), Yonkers (Westchester), Hempstead, and West Hempstead (Nassau) are homes to relatively noteworthy Haitian communities.

ADDITIONAL DEMOGRAPHIC DISTRIBUTION

The Haitian population in the United States is very diversified in terms of educational and skill levels, as well as socioeconomic status. The earlier waves were better educated and came from urban Haiti; consequently, in time members of this group managed to achieve solid middle-class status in the United States and to move to thriving areas (neighborhoods, suburbs, and counties) less populated by Haitians. For example, generally speaking, in New York, one finds more affluent Haitians in the neighborhoods of Holliswood and Long Island. In the Miami area, some reside in several northern sections of Miami-Dade County such as North Miami, Miami Shores, El Portal, and Miami Gardens; others in the southwest neighborhoods of Kendall and Coral Gables; and others in the middle-class sections of Broward County (such as Boca Raton and Plantation). In Chicago, they are scattered throughout the most prosperous sections of the city or they tend to establish their niches in the West suburbs. In Boston, they reside in the suburbs of Milton, Randolph, and Canton. According to estimates provided by community leaders in the course of fieldwork, approximately one-fifth (or slightly less) of the total Haitian population can be considered a solid middle class. Members of this group are for the most part professionals, with university degrees, who are employed in their fields—medicine, nursing, health related professions, law, education, journalism, engineering, social work, business, accounting, computer science—along with other managerial and administrative positions. A limited number comprises the owners of small- (possibly medium-) sized enterprises (restaurants, stores, travel agencies, real estate agencies, and the like).

However, there seems to be a consensus that the majority of the Haitian immigrant population currently residing in the United States belongs in the lower middle class and the working class. In Miami, Little Haiti is undoubtedly home to the largest working-class segment. In New York, the borough of Brooklyn has the largest concentration of more modest-income Haitian immigrants. In Boston, the neighborhoods of Mattapan and Dorchester house important working-class communities. In Chicago, working-class Haitians are scattered on both the North and South sides; in addition, one also finds a sizeable number in the adjacent city of Evanston. Many members of this group work mostly in the service industry, hotels, restaurants, hospitals, and nursing homes; others hold janitorial and craft/maintenance positions; and some (men for the most part) are taxi drivers. In short, they are part of the blue-collar workforce.

Table 4.8
Percentage of Haitian Immigrant Population under 40
for Selected Years

Year	Total number	Under 40	Percentage
1987	14,819	12,845	86.6%
1988	34,806	20,436	58.7%
1991	47,527	35,562	74.8%
1994	13,333	10,167	76.2%
1996	18,336	14,751	80.4%
1999	16,532	12,496	75.5%
2000	22,364	16,130	72.1%

Relatively speaking, the Haitian diaspora is rather young, with the majority under 40 years of age. To have an informed perspective on the age patterns of legal Haitian immigrants, let us look at the numbers provided by the INS for selected years. For the sake of clarity, these patterns are represented in Table 4.8. The overwhelming majority of the remaining age brackets is located within the group 40 to 50 years of age. Finally, it is also interesting to know that the female population is a bit higher than the male (with a difference of 11% or so). For example, in 1999, the female percentage was 55.5 percent; and in 2000, 56.4 percent. This pattern is similar to that of other immigrant groups who also have a larger female population.

CLIMATE OF RECEPTION

According to immigration patterns, the bulk of the Haitian population settled in the United States from the early 1980s onward (roughly 320,000 immigrants, based on official numbers). It was also the time when substantial numbers of boat people entered the southern Florida waters and started attracting strong resentment from the conservative sectors of the U.S. population and government. The story of the boat people is worth telling, as it is embedded in U.S. immigration policies and has attracted considerable media coverage, thus making it an American story.

The Boat People

Perhaps, it is through the saga of the boat people that the climate of reception toward Haitians can be most objectively assessed, since it involved well documented immigration policies and received the attention of important organizations, such as the NAACP, the Congressional Black Caucus, among other human rights organizations. Since the late 1970s and early 1980s, Haitian refugees have been considered to be "economic" rather than "political" refugees, as the United States ignored the correlation between the political situation and the economic conditions of Haiti. The government's position is clearly articulated in statements made in 1980 by John Bushnell, deputy assistant secretary for inter-American affairs, before the Subcommittee of Immigration of the House Judiciary Committee: "The stark contrast between living conditions and economic prospects in Haiti and the United States is the principal factor motivating emigration to this country."[10] Consequently, the U.S. government decided that Haitian refugees should be sent back home; thousands of cases seeking admission were denied. However, several human rights organizations, including religious organizations regrouped under the National Council of Churches (NCC), rejected the government's position, and vehemently urged President Carter to grant political asylum to the 8,000 refugees who had come since 1972. In a study completed by the NCC, it was reported that "the U.S. Government's position toward Haitian refugees contrasts sharply with the warm welcome extended to Cuban refugees (who are mostly whites) and to refugees from left wing dictatorships."[11] A class action suit was brought against the INS by the Haitian Refugee Center on behalf of 4,000 Haitians. The *Haitian Refugee Center v. Civiletti* story was covered in the July 3, 1980, issue of the *Washington Post* in an article titled "Haitians Win Round on U.S. Asylum." In his opinion statement, Judge King declared that the Immigration and Naturalization Service had followed a "systematic program designed to deport them [the Haitians] irrespective of their asylum claims."[12] The judge further observed that "those Haitians who came to the United States seeking freedom and justice did not find it. Instead they were confronted with an Immigration and Naturalization Service determined to deport them."[13] He also alluded to discrimination against Haitians on the part of the federal government, when comparing the treatment reserved to Cubans to that given to Haitians.

Just as the human rights organizations, African American leaders and civil rights activists also became vocal in the matter of the Haitian boat people. In the words of Congresswoman Shirley Chisholm of New York, who chaired the Congressional Black Caucus's Task Force on Haitian Refugees, they pressured the U.S. government, and INS in particular, "to adhere to this nation's fundamental tradition of equal protection for all persons under law by granting work authorization and due process to Haitians seeking political asylum in this country."[14] Other members of the Congressional Black Caucus, including Congressman Walter Fauntroy of the District of Columbia and Mickey Leland of Texas, argued that the government's handling of Haitian refugees was in violation of its open-door policy, and of the U.N. protocol regarding the status of refugees. In a similar manner, the NAACP vehemently registered its opposition against the double standard of treatment of Cubans and Haitians, and demanded that the government be fair in its immigration policies. As Benjamin Hooks, executive secretary of the association, wrote in a letter to President Reagan, "the action is clearly discriminatory, because it amplifies a pattern which, for the past five years, has singled out Haitian refugees for special and harsh treatment unlike any other refugees and in spite of the fact that we have welcomed and supported more than half million refugees from elsewhere in the past two years."[15] Expressing the same anger, civil rights activists joined in the fight for Haitian refugees. Reverend Jesse Jackson, speaking out at a protest rally in Miami in April 1980, made the following statement reported in the April 20 issue of the *Washington Post* of that year: "There is room in the United States for Cubans trying to escape oppression. There is room for Haitians trying to escape oppression." All these documented events go a long way to show that the Haitian immigration experience has been fraught with discrimination and prejudice from the time their significant presence was recorded on the shores of the United States.

All throughout the late eighties, the nineties, and to the present day, Haitian refugees continued to suffer extreme hardships from the Immigration and Naturalization Service, which tightened its laws in 1986 by enacting the Immigration Reform and Control Act (IRCA), and subsequently in 1996 by promulgating the Illegal Immigration Reform and Immigrant Responsibility Act (see chapter 1). Consequently, the fate of the boat people worsened. Some professionals and middle-class Haitian Americans began organizing themselves as associations and coalitions prepared to fight for the rights of Haitian refugees. Pressure from Haitian American organizations, such as the National Coalition for Haitian Rights (established in New York in 1982 as the National Coalition for Haitian Refugees) and the Haitian American Grassroots Coalition (based in Miami), along with several American human rights organizations, the Congressional Black Caucus, and several members of the Florida State Legislature—among them Congresswoman Carrie Meek—led to the passage of the Haitian Refugee Immigration Fairness Act

(HRIFA) of 1998 under the Clinton administration. However, in 2000 under the Bush administration, the INS issued a new policy requiring Haitian refugees (only Haitian refugees) to be detained in government facilities instead of releasing them to family members while they prepare their political asylum applications. The rationale offered was to deter further contingents from surging into this country. Subsequent to this policy, illegal Haitians intercepted at sea were rounded up in federal detention centers where allegations of their mistreatment surfaced. Indeed, it has been reported in the Haitian diasporic media, the *Haitian Times* in particular, that Haitian women, who had been held in the Krome Processing Center—since December 3, 2001, when their boat carrying 167 people was seized by the U.S. Coast Guard off the shores of southern Florida—complained that the guards sexually harassed them. These women were later transferred to the Turner Guilford Knight Correctional Center, a maximum-security prison in Miami, where the conditions of the inmates are said to be horrible, according to the testimony of these Haitian women themselves. The latest INS policy regarding Haitians has met with a great deal of resentment on the part of the Haitian community, American human rights advocates (Black and White), and the democratic sector of the U.S. government. In fact, a law suit was filed against the INS by the Florida Immigrant Advocacy Center in March 2002, alleging that the policy is discriminatory, since it applies only to Haitian refugees. Furthermore, demonstrations have been held in front of the U.S. Immigration and Naturalization Service buildings in Miami, New York, and Boston to urge President Bush and Attorney General Ashcroft to repeal this policy. Demonstrators included such American notables as actor Danny Glover, Florida State Representative Frederica Wilson, Cheryl Little, executive director of the Florida Immigrant Advocacy Center, in addition to well-known Haitian advocates such as Dina Paul-Parks, former executive director of the National Coalition for Haitian Rights (2002–2003); Massachusetts House Representative Marie St. Fleur; Marleine Bastien, executive director of the Haitian Women Center in Miami; and Gespie Metellus, executive director of the Haitian Neighborhood Center, among several others.[16] Moreover, after the latest group of boat people was apprehended in late October 2002, more protests followed in Miami and New York with the same indignation.[17] Such public events occurring in major metropolitan areas convincingly attest to the lack of welcome Haitians find in the United States. No Haitian, no matter the level of socioeconomic success achieved in the United States, can really remain aloof from or impervious to such a negative climate, where Haitian immigrants are constantly seen as a problem for American society.

African American actor Danny Glover demonstrating with Haitian immigrants in Miami. Courtesy of the *Haitian Times.*

Perhaps more than any other group, Haitian immigrants became the victims of strong attacks, the more ferocious of these being their characterization as AIDS carriers. Indeed on March 4, 1983, the U.S. Centers for Disease Control (CDC) identified four AIDS high-risk groups: homosexuals, Haitians, hemophiliacs, and heroin users, thus imposing membership into this infamous "Four-H-Club" on Haitians. Following the CDC's exclusionary lead, the United States Public Health Service recommended that Haitians not donate blood, and, in consequence, school blood drives blatantly excluded Haitian teenagers. Those recommendations were taken seriously, and the Food and Drug Administration (FDA) issued an original stipulation preventing Haitians who had come to the United States after 1977 from donating blood. The discriminatory policies did not stop there, and in February 1990, the FDA's paranoia reached its climax when this time it issued a ruling prohibiting *all* Haitians from giving blood. Protest demonstrations were organized by outraged Haitian immigrant communities in New York, Boston, Miami, and Washington, urging the "Federal *Discrimination* Agency" to fight "AIDS, not nationality."[18] The strongest of these

Haitians demonstrating in front of the Immigration and Naturalization Service
Building in Miami. Courtesy of the *Haitian Times*.

protests took place on Friday, April 20, 1990, in New York City; it was a
demonstration march that attracted thousands of Haitians, as well as many
other concerned Americans (Blacks and Whites) and other groups. This
demonstration received extensive coverage in the *New York Times*. Indeed, its
April 21, 1990, issue reported that "tens of thousands of demonstrators
swarmed across the Brooklyn Bridge in lower Manhattan to protest a Federal Health policy on blood donations that they say unfairly stigmatized
Haitians and Africans." The article went on to say that the march started
from Cadman Plaza in Brooklyn and ended at the Federal Plaza in Manhattan "with a crowd that the police estimated at 50,000 and that rally organizers said was nearly 80,000." As a result of such a manifestation of anger, the
FDA rescinded the ban on Haitians in December 1990, allowing them to be
potential donors.

The effects of those accusations were devastating for Haitian immigrants:
prospective employers did not feel it was safe to hire Haitians; walls were
spray painted with signs denigrating Haitians; Haitian store owners endured
bankruptcy; Haitian families were evicted from their homes; and Haitian

Three leading Haitian women activists, Léonie Hermantin (from the Haitian Neighborhood Center), Marleine Bastien (from the Haitian Women Center of Miami), and Gepsie Metellus (from the Haitian Neighborhood Center), attend a Haitian American Grassroots Coalition meeting in Miami. Courtesy of the *Haitian Times*.

children were mistreated in school by their peers and humiliated by their teachers.[19] In fact, several second-generation Haitian immigrants have reported that, during the 1980s and early 1990s, they were afraid of telling their peers at school that they were Haitians for fear of being assaulted, as such assaults were endured by newcomers who could not pass as something else. Many Haitian children were ridiculed and called by all sorts of names. Others were severely beaten up in the bathrooms or the hallways. To this day, many Haitians tell endless stories of discrimination encountered in the course of their daily lives. These include being passed over for promotion, having their applications for housing rejected even though they qualified, being pulled over by the police for no apparent reason, unnecessary delays at obtaining service in public agencies, excessive rudeness on the part of White bosses, and reluctance on the part of realtors to show them houses in predominantly White neighborhoods.[20]

Currently, there is a strong feeling in the Haitian immigrant community that the United States is falling short of its promise of equality and justice for all. Many members of the community perceive that race is a factor in the way they are perceived by American society at large. As evidence of this, Haitians allude to the better treatment reserved for Cubans under the "wet foot–dry foot policy," which automatically grants asylum to any Cuban who manages to disembark onto U.S. shores and to the willingness of the U.S. government to recognize individuals from certain Eastern European countries—Bosnia-Herzegovina and Yugoslavia, for example—as being political instead of economic refugees. Indeed, fieldwork conducted with Haitian immigrants—particularly community advocates—in several metropolitan areas convincingly underscores the community's desire to make the U.S. government understand that the political climate, which prevents the development of a stable economic environment, drives migration from Haiti. As many members of the community contend, the Haitian refugee problem is a political problem; Haitians who seek asylum in the United States are political refugees who should not be locked up. In the words of Gepsie Metellus, executive director of the Haitian Neighborhood Center, the Haitian problem "is simple. Free them [the refugees]. Haitians are not terrorists."[21]

The Abner Louima Story

While the fate of the latest waves of Haitian refugees remains to be determined by the Immigration and Naturalization Service, the experience of the legal population is also fraught with instances of prejudice and constant hardships. In recent times, the most abominable of these is the Abner Louima case, demonstrating police brutality against Haitian immigrants in New York City. This case attracted national attention and made headline news. Perhaps some of the readers might have followed it on CNN, since the case went to court. Louima's defense team included prominent defense attorney Johnnie Cochran, Jr., whom many may remember from the O. J. Simpson trial. Given the level of publicity this incident received, some details are appropriate.[22] On Saturday, August 9, 1997, around four o'clock in the morning, Abner Louima, after having spent the night at the Haitian Rendez-Vous club located on Flatbush Avenue in Brooklyn, New York, came out and witnessed a fight between two women. Someone in the club called the police, who dispatched a squad car from Brooklyn's 70th Precinct. Louima reported that the cops began pushing people around, shouting racial slurs, calling them "niggers," and asking, "Why do you people come to this country if you cannot speak English?" He also said that he did not think he was involved in the incident since he had been "just a by-stander watching events." In Louima's own words, this is what happened:

Haitian victim of police brutality Abner Louima with his
attorney, Johnny Cochran, Jr. Courtesy of the *Haitian Times*.

A cop pushed me to the ground and handcuffed my hands. Two cops
put me in their patrol car and drove me to the corner of Glenwood and
Nostrand. There was another car there. They kicked and beat me with
their radios. They were yelling, "You people can't even talk English. I
am going to teach you to respect a cop." None of the cops had their
nametags on. They put me back in the car and drove me to the corner
of Glenwood and Bedford. They met two other cops and beat me again.
This time in the legs too.[23]

Louima's nightmare was just beginning, as he was now taken to the 70th
Precinct by the four cops involved in the successive beatings. The policemen
were later identified as Justin Volpe, Charles Schwartz, Thomas Wiese, and
Thomas Bruder. They arrived with their battered victim at the precinct

around 4:50 A.M. It is reported that the police stripped Louima from the waist down supposedly in order to search for weapons and drugs. Again, here is Louima in his own words:

> My pants were down at my ankles, in full view of the other cops. They walked me over to the bathroom and closed the door. There were two cops. One said, "You niggers have to learn to respect police officers." The other one said, "If you yell or make any noise, I will kill you." Then one held me and the other stuck a plunger up my behind. He pulled it out and shoved it in my mouth, broke my teeth and said, "That's your shit, nigger."[24]

Around eight o'clock, Louima was taken to Coney Island Hospital. Doctors found that his small intestine was torn, his bladder perforated, his front teeth broken, his body completely bruised and lacerated. It took several lengthy operations, some two months apart, to repair the physical damage done to the Haitian immigrant by the New York City police.

From 1999 to 2002, a series of trials occurred. In 1999, Justin Volpe pleaded guilty to sodomizing Louima and was sentenced to 30 years in prison, a term that he is currently serving. Schwartz was tried for civil rights violations; Wiese and Bruder for perjury and conspiracy to obstruct justice. The former received a 15-year sentence, and the latter two each received a 5-year sentence but were freed on bond pending appeal. All three officers appealed their sentences. On February 28, 2002, they won their appeals, and their convictions were overturned. More legal brouhaha followed. A new trial began for Schwartz on June 24, 2002; on July 16, 2002, the jury found him guilty of perjury but was deadlocked on the civil-rights-violation charges. In a plea bargain that took place on September 2002, Schwartz pleaded guilty to perjury and all the other charges were dropped; he agreed to serve a 5-year sentence. It appears that Wiese and Bruder will not be tried again. In the midst of these criminal trials, Louima filed a civil suit that was settled out of court. On July 12, 2001, he accepted a settlement of $8.7 million from the City of New York and the police union. Louima now lives in Miami, where he is an advocate for Haitian refugees. In Miami in early June 2002, Louima was part of a small delegation of individuals who went to visit the Haitian refugees held in the Krome Processing Center and at the Turner Guilford Knight Correctional Center. At the time, Reverend Al Sharpton was in Miami and wanted to express his indignation at the INS discriminatory policy. Therefore, at the initiative of Florida State Representative Frederica Wilson, a delegation was put together to accompany Reverend Sharpton to the detention facilities on June 4, 2002. In addition to Louima, Representative Wilson, and Reverend Sharpton, this delegation included Marleine Bastien (executive director of the Haitian Women Center), Cheryl Little (executive director of the Florida Immigrant Advocacy Center), and several members of the Haitian Lawyers Association, among others.

Moreover, other instances of police brutality against Haitian immigrants have been documented. On January 16, 2002, 23-year-old Georgy Louisgene was gunned down by the police in a Brooklyn project. The event received a great deal of coverage in the *Haitian Times* (January 23–29 and February 6–12, 2003, issues). The young man died two days before he was slated to take the U.S. citizenship exam. In an encounter with the police for reasons that remained unclear, police fired eight shots, five of which fatally hit him. Community organizations were outraged that the police could not subdue the 115-pound young man, who was not carrying a gun, without resorting to such excessive force. They saw in their actions another instance of racial and ethnic discrimination. All these events go a long way to illustrate that the relationship between law enforcement officers and Haitians in predominantly Haitian neighborhoods have been riddled with conflicts.

In short, many Haitians, whether in New York, Miami, Boston, or Chicago, have a story to tell about the prejudice and discrimination they, themselves, or a friend or family member, have encountered in the United States. Collectively, these stories paint the compelling portrait of a people who have come from a different shore in search of a better life. In their quest for prosperity, Haitian immigrants' dreams and aspirations often clash with the realities of their new world. Faced with the complexities of race, ethnicity, labor market, and social structure in American society, Haitian immigrants have come to develop mechanisms of adjustment and adaptation to their new surroundings. The following chapters explore in detail those mechanisms.

NOTES

1. Ferguson (1987: 57–58).
2. As reported in Pamphile (2001: 175).
3. Ferguson (1987: 64). See also Stepick (1986: 11).
4. As reported in Pamphile (2001: 176).
5. The 2000 *Statistical Yearbook* is the latest available at the time of this writing.
6. As quoted in the *Haitian Times* (November 27–December 3, 2002, p. 7).
7. In New York City Department of City Planning (1992: 32).
8. In Massachusetts Office of Refugee and Immigrant Health (1998: chapter on Haitians). The report is not paginated.
9. In Boston Redevelopment Authority (1999: 4, 6). Haiti is followed by China, Ireland, Dominican Republic, and Italy.

10. As quoted in Pamphile (2001: 176).

11. As quoted in Miller (1984: 93).

12. As quoted in Pamphile (2001: 177).

13. As quoted in Miller (1984: 94).

14. As quoted in Pamphile (2001: 178).

15. Miller (1984: 96).

16. While doing fieldwork in Boston in July 2002, I had the opportunity to attend a protest rally held at midday in front of the INS building. Joining the Haitian cause, White members of the Massachusetts Immigrant and Refugee Coalition and of the Irish Immigrant Centre joined their Haitian fellow Bostonians in their demand for social justice and chanted with them: "INS: We're not less," and "Equal treatment for Haitian refugees."

17. For more on these demonstrations, see the *Haitian Times* (May 8–14, 2002; July 31–August 6, 2002; and November 6–12, 2002). See also the *Boston Haitian Reporter* (August 2002).

18. Farmer (1992: 218–19).

19. Ibid., p. 214.

20. This information was reported to me during interviews in the course of my fieldwork.

21. Quoted in the *Haitian Times* (May 8–14, 2002, front page).

22. Some of the Louima information has appeared in Zéphir (2001: 37–38). However, the more recent information comes from various media sources, including CNN and the *Haitian Times*.

23. As reported in *Haiti Progrès* (August 20–26, 1997, Volume 15, p. 22).

24. Ibid.

5

No Longer Invisible: Haitian Ethnic Communities

While it is a documented fact that Haitian immigrants have experienced a great deal of discrimination upon arrival in the United States, they nevertheless have chosen not to return to their home country. Instead they are determined to beat the odds and find the path to economic stability and freedom, so deeply associated with the United States, which calls itself "the land of the free and the home of the brave." This fact alone can attest to the magnitude of the political and economic problems that plague Haiti and the resolve of Haitian immigrants to live free of oppression, as was discussed in detail in previous chapters. Haitians make a conscious choice to leave behind the experienced political tyranny and life of suffering; they reach for a land of opportunity where their hopes and aspirations can be realized. They are optimistic that the United States will, in the end, keep its promise of equality and justice for all. They believe in the democratic ideals upon which this country was founded; they believe in its humanitarian traditions. Even those held in detention centers hope that they will eventually be granted asylum and allowed to begin new lives here, as free people. In short, Haitian immigrants believe in the message contained in Emma Lazarus's poem *The New Colossus,* for it symbolizes what the United States represents to every single immigrant who yearns to escape the miseries and despair of the past to embrace a new ideal for the future. This ideal is embedded in American freedom, success, and happiness:

Give me your tired, your poor,
Your huddled masses yearning to breathe free,

The wretched refuse of your teeming shore,
Send these, the homeless, tempest-tossed to me,
I lift my lamps beside the golden door!

Emma Lazarus's famous words, permanently placed over the Statue of Liberty's main entrance, are indelibly engraved into the collective immigrant memory. As America's new immigrants, Haitians have been attracted by the message of the Statue of Liberty; all of them have come to the United States to escape persecution, tyranny, and poverty, to survive, and to create a new life full of opportunities. Regardless of the initial climate of reception, they develop mechanisms of adjustment and adaptation to their land of resettlement. More important, they have the will and determination to endure and to ensure a better future for their offspring.

Haitian immigrants have established their communities in the northeast, principally in the New York and Boston metropolitan areas; in South Florida; and to a smaller extent in the Midwest. In the following pages, representative Haitian ethnic communities in New York, Miami, Boston, and Chicago will be discussed in an attempt to offer a panoramic view of Haitian diasporic life in the United States. Additionally, collective efforts undertaken by the Haitian diaspora to improve its community image will be addressed.

A TALE OF FOUR CITIES

New York

New York City has the largest concentration of Haitians in the country as well as the oldest established Haitian communities of the four urban centers under discussion. As stated before, the conservative estimate of the legal Haitian population in the New York City metropolitan area, as recorded by the INS, is approximately 156,000. However, community leaders and directors of community centers, who come in constant contact with the illegal population, strongly believe that the actual number is closer to 400,000, including the nonimmigrant and undocumented entrants, as well as the legal population who do not fill out the census forms. Moreover, the New York City Haitian population represents a very heterogeneous group, reflecting the various strata of Haitian society. Older members of the middle class came during the U.S. occupation in the 1930s and 1940s; at the time they established their enclaves in Harlem, where they mingled with African Americans and other Caribbean immigrants who were contributing to the Harlem Renaissance. Significant waves followed exponentially during the Duvalier era that started in 1957 and ended in 1986 with the ousting of Baby Doc. These waves were more heterogeneous than previous ones, as no single class of Haitians was immune from the Duvaliers' dictatorship. To date, cohorts of Haitians continue to come to New York, many being sent for by relatives already established in the city.

Haitians reside in all the boroughs, but the largest communities are found in Brooklyn, where the legal population is placed at approximately 88,763, and in Queens, where the number of Haitians is believed to be around 40,000. Members of the community who are of working-class background tend to establish their residence in Brooklyn, primarily in the neighborhoods of Flatbush, Crown Heights, East Flatbush, and Vanderveer; they are apartment dwellers. Middle-class Haitians who choose to stay in Brooklyn own brownstone homes in the Park Slope area and single-family homes in the Midwood section. Generally speaking, Haitians themselves consider the majority of their compatriots living in Queens to be mostly middle class. Members of this group enjoy ownership of their homes or cooperative apartments in the neighborhoods of Cambria Heights, Queens Village, Springfield Gardens, and Jamaica. Less-privileged Haitians settle in the working-class neighborhoods of Jackson Heights; generally members of the professional community live in the more affluent section of Holliswood, and some move to the adjacent counties of Nassau and Suffolk, which are parts of Long Island. The number of Haitians living in Nassau and Suffolk counties is estimated at 25,000 to 30,000. In Manhattan, a small concentration of working-class Haitians (7%) congregates on the Upper West Side and Harlem. Some reside along Cathedral Parkway and in Washington Heights. Very few Haitians (less than 1%) establish their niches in the Bronx. In this discussion, it is also important to recall that Haitians have established communities in the neighboring counties of Westchester and Rockland, which are included in the greater New York metropolitan statistical area. In fact, Spring Valley in Rockland County has a relatively large segment of the New York population, estimated at close to 20,000. Moreover, in 2001, a Haitian, Margareth Jourdan, was sworn in as the first Black woman to serve as a village justice for Spring Valley. Haitians are very proud of her as she is the first Haitian American to be appointed judge and also the first Haitian American to serve in the capacity of a highly visible government official for the state of New York. In June 2003, the city council of the neighboring city of East Orange, New Jersey, confirmed the nomination of another Haitian American woman, Sybil Elias, as municipal court judge. In a similar connection, one can mention that another Haitian, Dr. Jacques Jiha, serves as deputy comptroller for New York State, in charge of pension investment and bonds placement, after having held a similar post for both New York City and Nassau County. These events

Spring Valley Village Justice Margareth Jourdan, being
sworn-in in June 2001 by New York State Governor
George Pataki. Courtesy of the *Haitian Times.*

demonstrate that Haitian Americans in New York (and New Jersey) are gradually making their way into mainstream America and are qualified to hold
senior level positions in government.

The sheer number of Haitians in New York makes them a highly visible
ethnic community. Indeed, the Haitian presence is real and cannot go unno-
ticed by anyone, even the tourist who visits the Big Apple for the first time.
That tourist has a strong chance of being taken from the airport to his or her
destination by a Haitian cab driver. Moreover, individuals using taxis on a
daily basis, whether in Manhattan, Queens, or Brooklyn, have more than
likely come in contact with Haitian cabbies. A good number of working-class
Haitians make a living in the taxi service. In their ethnic neighborhoods, Haitians have managed to visibly recreate the cultural habits of their homeland

with the establishment of many ethnic businesses, such as music shops, grocery stores, restaurants, bakeries, bars, beauty and barber shops, travel agencies, shipping companies, money transfer companies, and a hodgepodge of other businesses, which prominently display their allegiances to their native country.[1] Those are found all along Flatbush, Church, and Nostrand avenues, as well as along Eastern Parkway in Brooklyn; on Linden, Farmers and Francis Lewis boulevards, and Jamaica and Hillside avenues in Queens. They are easily recognizable since many display signs written both in English and Haitian Creole (sometimes in French), such as *Yoyo Fritaille, Le Manoir, Le Viconte, Haiti Parcel & Cargo Inc., Bakery Creole, Chez Nemours, La Patisserie, Sanon's Bargain Center,* and *Soleil Plus, Inc.* On intensely hot days, passersby strolling along these avenues and boulevards have their nostrils filled with the aromas of fried pork meat *(griyo),* fried plantains *(bannann peze),* and rice and beans *(diri kole ak pwa),* and their ears with rhythms of Sweet Micky, Konpa, Zin, T-Vice, Carimi, Tabou Combo, and Boukman Eksperyans, to name some of the most celebrated musical groups and bands. Animated conversations in Haitian Creole can be heard, as members of the community "hang out" in those shops and businesses to discuss home politics and news, exchange gossip, find out what goes on in the community, and keep alive their various traditions, be they culinary, intellectual, literary, or artistic.

Along with their various ethnic businesses in New York City, Haitians have established their own community media—newspapers, radio, and television—that keep them informed of daily events in the Haitian diaspora and in the homeland. Major Haitian newspapers produced in New York include the *Haitian Times, Haïti Observateur,* and *Haïti Progrès,* all located in Brooklyn. The *Haitian Times* is probably the best known of the Haitian diasporic papers. It is published weekly and has a wide readership all throughout the diaspora; it is also very comprehensive in its coverage of Haitian matters both in New York and Haiti, and elsewhere. Moreover, it is an outlet chosen by Haitian businesses as well as several U.S. agencies to advertise their services. In the community, there are four Haitian radio stations that function on a 24-hour basis: Radio Tropicale, Radio Soleil, Radio Lakay, and Radyo Pa Nou. *Perspectives Haïtiennes, Moment Creole,* which receives some airtime from the leading Black radio station in New York City (WLIB), and *Radio Sanba* are among the most-listened-to radio programs. *Haiti Dyaspo* and *La Lanterne Haïtienne* are widely watched news magazine programs. Furthermore, Haitian immigrants in New York have formed several service organizations and community centers that are critical to the diffusion of Haitian culture and values. The best known of these is the Haitian Centers Council, Inc., established in 1982 and based in Brooklyn, which maintains under its purview eight centers located throughout the New York metropolitan area. Four are located in Brooklyn (the Flatbush Haitian Center is the better known in Brooklyn); one in Queens (the Haitian American United for Progress Community Center, or HAUP); one in Manhattan (the Haitian Neighborhood Service Center); one in Spring Valley (Rockland County); and the other also within the Greater New York metropolitan area. These centers focus on immigration, refugee assistance, employment, and job training matters, housing assistance, youth and family services, health education, as well as on cultural enrichment activities. The Haitian American Alliance is also well-known in the community for its advocacy, civil and social services; so is *Dwa Fanm* (Women's Rights), which focuses on women's issues. Another important agency is the National Coalition for Haitian Rights (NCHR), which deals with matters of immigration, welfare, and legal rights of Haitian immigrants. This organization played a vital role in mobilizing the community in the Abner Louima case, described in chapter 4. Moreover, NCHR is very involved in the matter of the latest groups of Haitian boat people and is fighting with the INS for their release from the detention centers.

The religious needs of the community are met by several Catholic and Protestant churches throughout the city. For example, Catholic masses in Haitian Creole are conducted at St. Jerome Church and at St. Theresa of Avila in Brooklyn and at Sacred Heart Church in Cambria Heights in Queens. Haitian Protestant churches are more numerous and are found all over Brooklyn and Queens. Further, practitioners of the Vodou religion can go to a host of Vodou priests and priestesses—called *oungans* and *manbos,* respectively, by Haitians—who minister to their spiritual needs. Some use the basements of their homes as sanctuaries or temples for worship, while others rent spaces from large apartment houses to conduct their ministries. The best known of Haitian Vodou priestesses or *manbos* is undoubtedly Mama Lola, who resides in Brooklyn. She is regarded as a healer, who performs "treatments" on those in need. In fact, Mama Lola has been the object of scholarly research: Karen McCarthy Brown, for instance, wrote extensively about her in a book titled *Mama Lola: A Vodou Priestess in Brooklyn.*[2] Hundreds of Haitians pour into these converted basement temples to seek the assistance of the *lwas* or Vodou spirits capable of healing their suffering.

For their social and recreational needs, Haitians have formed a variety of clubs and associations that enable them to carry on many of the social practices of the homeland. Many of these clubs tend to have members who come from the same hometown in Haiti. Those clubs include Primevère (whose membership consists of people from Cap-Haitien), La Solidarité Jacmélienne (comprised of people from the city of Jacmel), Casegha, and L'Anolis Vert. On special occasions, such as Christmas, New Year's Eve, and Carnival, to name just these three, special events—particularly dances—are organized and attract a relatively large number of Haitians who come to enjoy and dance to the lively music provided by such Haitian bands as Tabou Combo or Boukman Eksperyans. Other organizations have a professional orientation; their membership consists of Haitians sharing the same profession, for example, the Haitian American Law Enforcement Fraternal Organization (HALEFO), or the association of nurses, of engineers, of social workers, and so forth. Some have a literary or historical orientation. One such organization is the Fondation Mémoire, whose mission, as the name might suggest, is to keep alive the history of Haiti and to contribute to the preservation of the Haitian cultural patrimony.

Although Haitians are employed in all sectors of the city, there are some businesses and agencies that hire a significant number of Haitians. Therefore, Haitians do have the opportunity to have fellow Haitians as coworkers and colleagues. This situation can be very beneficial to them, as it tempers the sometimes hostile workplace. For example, it is not unusual to find several Haitians working in the same hospital, as nurses, as nurses' aides, and in other staff or custodial positions. The same situation obtains in banks and insurance companies. The United Nations also hires Haitians for a variety of clerical, secretarial, and administrative positions, owing to their bilingual ability in French and English, which makes them competitive workers in international organizations. Moreover, there is a consensus that the New York City Board of Education is an agency where a great many Haitians have been able to find good employment opportunities. The large number of Haitian students attending the New York City public schools, particularly in Brooklyn, has compelled the board of education to hire Haitian teachers and guidance counselors who can address the needs of this particular student clientele. Many of these educators are used in bilingual education programs (Creole and English) that are designed to help Haitian children with limited English proficiency; a few have risen to the coveted positions of principals and assistant principals. Indeed, significant numbers of Haitian students are enrolled at PS17 and PS189 (Brooklyn); George Wood Wingate High School located in the East Flatbush neighborhood; Erasmus Hall High School located in Flatbush; John Dewey High School, Clara Barton High School, and Midwood High School, also in Brooklyn; and Springfield Gardens High School in Queens, to name several schools. In addition, a relatively large number of college-age Haitian students attend the local colleges of the City University of New York (CUNY), in particular Brooklyn College and Kingborough

Community College in Brooklyn; Queens College and York College in Queens; City College and Hunter College in Manhattan. In these and other institutions (including New York University), Haitian students have formed their own Haitian student associations, which are very active in promoting Haitian culture and are responsible for bringing to campus notable Haitians and Haitian Americans—writers, educators, political activists, journalists, and others. CUNY has on its faculty a few Haitian professors and instructors who regularly teach courses about Haitian history, culture, language, literature, and linguistics.

Haitians, thanks to the wide variety of ethnic affairs—businesses, media, churches and temples, community centers, social and professional associations, musical and other artistic activities—they manage to create, have been able to transplant a great deal of their homeland traditions in New York City. It is this transplantation of Haitian lifestyle that helps many of them survive the hardships of immigration, and the hostility of the surrounding milieu. In so doing, they have undoubtedly added their colors to the great American kaleidoscope.

Bob's Classic Barber Shop on Church Avenue in Brooklyn, NY. Courtesy of the *Haitian Times*.

Miami

The legal Haitian population of Miami-Dade County, based on government records, is approximately 100,000. However, when one factors in the under-representation of the census data for a variety of reasons discussed earlier, as well as the number of illegal immigrants, there is good reason to believe that community leaders and technocrats who work with the Haitian community are not wrong to place the county's Haitian population at over 200,000. Miami is an interesting city in that it continuously replenishes itself with Haitian immigrants, in addition to a host of other ethnic groups from the Caribbean and Latin America. On the one hand, a large contingent of Haitians is unquestionably the boat people, who have been steadily pouring onto the southern Florida shores since the early 1970s. They have established themselves in the Edison/Little River area of Miami, which eventually came to be referred to as Little Haiti. Once they are able, some end up moving out of Little Haiti to the neighboring municipality of North Miami, where a relatively large segment of Haitian immigrants of lower-middle-class background relocates. On the other hand, Miami is also experiencing another wave of Haitian immigration, this time coming from the Northeast United States (New York and Boston), the Midwest (Chicago), and Montreal, Canada. The severity of the winters in those regions compels significant numbers of Haitians, who have not been able to adjust to the frigid climate, to seek warmer weather in the South. This particular group of Haitians is composed mostly of middle-class individuals who, having worked assiduously for many years, have been able to save money and profit from the sale of their homes in order to relocate to Miami, where the cost of living is lower than that of Boston and New York and where the tropical weather and lifestyle are reminiscent of those of their native Haiti. This class of Haitians lives in the middle-class sections of Miami Shores, North Miami Beach, El Portal, Miami Gardens, and the southwest neighborhoods of Kendall and Coral Gables. Most are employed in their professions as doctors, dentists, nurses, accountants, computer scientists, teachers, psychologists, managers, lawyers, engineers, social workers, and journalists. Some have solid jobs in city and state government offices or own their own businesses. In addition, one can find a few Haitians in higher education. There are a couple of Haitian university professors and administrators at Florida International University and the University of Miami, where many Haitian students go, in addition to Miami-Dade Community College.

Irrespective of the presence of middle-class Haitians, Miami is considered the city that received (and continues to receive) the largest segment of lower-class Haitians, consisting of poor peasants from *andeyò* (countryside) and

North Miami Mayor Joe Celestin at a Haitian Carnival celebration in Miami on April 13, 2003. Courtesy of the *Haitian Times*.

urban dwellers who were roaming the streets in search of *lavi* (life). Many of these Haitians found new lives in the Edison/Little River section of Miami, one of the oldest neighborhoods in the city, which the Whites deserted in the 1970s. Soon after, this area became known as Little Haiti and is now one of the most recognizable Haitian communities in the United States.[3] From north to south, Little Haiti extends from 84th Street to 36th Street; from west to east, it is 10 blocks wide, stretching from 6th Avenue NW to 4th Avenue NE. It is crossed by two major north-south axes: Miami Avenue and 2nd Avenue NE (called Avenue Morrisseau-Leroy after the well-known Haitian writer); 36th, 54th, 62nd, and 79th Streets are the main thoroughfares that cross east/west. Estimates of the population of Little Haiti vary from 40,000 to 55,000. Little Haiti is also considered one of the poorest areas of Miami-Dade County. The following figures were released by the Edison/Little River Neighborhood Planning Program (1994–1996): the per capita income is $5,693, the median household income is $14,142, and close to half the population lives below poverty level.[4] City government efforts are currently underway to revitalize the neighborhood, by creating long-term economic development, and improving housing and infrastructure. The City of Miami has established in Little Haiti a neighborhood service center (along with others throughout the metropolitan area), known as Neighborhood Enhancement Teams (NET) to address the social problems of the community

Most of the Haitian businesses are found along the major arterials mentioned above; like those of New York, they are unmistakably Haitian with names such as Bèl Fouchèt, Piman Bouk, Libreri Mapou, and Cayard Market. They include restaurants, grocery stores, dry-cleaning establishments, tailor and shoe repair shops, shipping and money transfer companies, and botanicas (shops that sell mostly religious/spiritual objects, including Vodou artifacts), among others. Little Haiti is home to two major schools whose student population is predominantly Haitian: Toussaint Louverture Elementary School (whose principal is Haitian) and Edison High School. Haitian students also attend Morningside Elementary School (whose principal is also Haitian), Little River Elementary School, Shadow Lawn Elementary School, Horace Mann Middle School, and North Miami High School (whose adult education program is headed by a Haitian). A Haitian-owned minibus company—Miami Mini-Bus—transports the Little Haitians throughout the area on *jetneys,* or vans. People familiar with this service say that on a daily basis, an average of 5,000 Haitians use these *jetneys.* Along with their various ethnic shops, the Haitian community of Miami has a variety of media. *Haiti en Marche,* a well-known diasporic paper with a wide circulation in New York, Boston, Montreal, and Port-au-Prince, is produced in Miami. Radio Carnivale is a Haitian-owned radio station that enjoys a wide audience among the South Florida Haitian community. *Piman Bouk, Pè Johnny,* and *Obri Blag* are popular radio programs. The Haitian Television Network is a station that caters to the Haitian community; so does Island TV, formerly called Island Magazine, which now operates a low power television station. Libreri Mapou, a well-established Haitian bookstore located in the heart of Little Haiti, carries quite an assortment of Haitian books, newspapers, and magazines, as well as Haitian artwork. One can also buy at the Libreri Mapou tickets to cultural events happening in the community; the owner, Jean Mapou, is a well-known community activist involved in a wide range of folkloric and cultural activities ranging from story telling, poetry recitation, dance shows, and the like. Jan Mapou is also the founder of the popular dance troupe Sosyete Koukouy (Firefly Society). Established in Miami in 1986, Sosyete Koukouy promotes folk art and traditional folk culture through the use of literature and dance. With regard to Haitian art, the famous Galerie d'Art Nader of longstanding tradition in Port-au-Prince has established a branch in Coral Gables in the southwest area of Miami. This particular location brings a great deal of visibility to Haitian art, since it is known for its reputable art galleries and is home to the Coral Gables Gallery Association, which organizes on every first Friday of the month a gallery night that attracts a good crowd. The association provides shuttles that pick up art lovers for a free tour of all member art galleries, including the Galerie d'Art Nader. This is undoubtedly a premier art gallery that prides itself with offering "the best variety of Haitian art around the world." The Jakmel Art Gallery and Culture Center located on Byscane Boulevard is another art establishment, which serves in addition as a place for worship. Indeed, in the back there is a Vodou temple that many Haitians attend regularly, the Caribbean Backyard, home of Papa Loko and Lwa Mistik. Other Vodou priests *(oungans)* and priestesses *(manbos)* conduct their services out of their homes, and they are known to the community where word of mouth or *teledyòl* is always a good source of information. Haitians of the Catholic faith go to Notre Dame Church, which oversees the Pierre Toussaint Haitian Catholic Center (named after the Black Saint of Saint-Domingan origin), or St. James Church. Other denominations—Protestant, Baptist, or Adventist—have several churches in Little Haiti and other municipalities with a significant Haitian population. Additionally, in North Miami there exists a well-regarded Haitian-owned medical center, the Comprehensive Health Center, that provides health care to a large number of Haitians. It focuses on general practice and, additionally, treats musculoskeletal injuries. This medical center also provides employment opportunities to Haitian health care professionals, and its director, Dr. Rudolph Moise, is well-known throughout the community for his philanthropic work. Finally, in the tourist and entertainment area of South Beach, one finds a very reputable Haitian restaurant named *Tap Tap* (after the colorful minivans used for local transportation in Port-au-Prince), that attracts not only middle-class Haitian clientele but also American and foreign customers. The owners, although non-Haitian, have spent a significant amount of time in Haiti; therefore, they endeavor to maintain the authenticity of the Haitian cuisine—thanks to Haitian chefs—and offer their facilities to serve the cultural needs of the Haitian community, which often hosts some of its functions at *Tap Tap.*

The proximity of Miami to Haiti, the constant comings and goings of Haitians, and the good weather make the community particularly keen on transplanting Haitian lifestyle and practices in this tropical U.S. city. The fact that Miami is not as big as New York, Boston, or Chicago seems to intensify movement among Haitians. Indeed, they travel lesser distances, live in closer proximity, and consequently are very easily able to stay in touch with, and participate in, the community's happenings, if they so choose. Many such activities are of a social nature, as Haitians are known for their love of music and dance. They are entertained by several Haitian American bands based in Miami, and others from New York and Haiti that come to perform at various times during the year. Moreover, there appears to be some level of civic engagement on the part of members of the community exemplified on the one hand by the number of community organizations that exist and their visibility throughout the city, and on the other by Haitian gains in local politics.[5] With regard to the former, there are several centers that are involved in various issues of community and economic development, legal and immigration advocacy, social service and health, and political activism. The oldest of these centers is the Haitian American Community Association of Dade (HACAD) founded in 1975, originally to help illegal Haitian students whom the school board did not want to accept in the public schools. Other well-known organizations include the Haitian Refugee Center, the Haitian American Grassroots Coalition, the Haitian American Foundation, Inc. (HAFI), the Haitian American Youth of Tomorrow (HAYOT), the Fanm Ayisyen Nan Miyami (FANM, Haitian Women of Miami), the Haitian Neighborhood Center (also known as *Sant La*), the Center for Haitian Studies (CHS), the Center of Information and Orientation, and the Society for Haitian Advancement, Recognition, and Education (SHARE), among several others. In addition to these social service–oriented centers, there exists quite a number of other professional and cultural organizations—such as, for example, the Society of Haitian American Professional and Entrepreneurs (SHAPE), the Haitian American Political Caucus, the Haitian Lawyers Association, the Haitian American Engineers and Scientists, and the Haitian American Historical Society (mentioned in chapter 1 for its work with Savannah officials to build a monument to commemorate the Haitian participation in the Battle of Savannah in 1779)—that promote the interests of Haitians.[6] With regard to local and state officials, Miami-Dade County and the state of Florida have the largest number of Haitians who have been elected to office: Josaphat (Joe) Célestin is the mayor of North Miami; Jacques Despinosse and Jean Monestime are councilmen, also in North Miami; Philippe Dérose, former vice-mayor of El Portal, is now city council-at-large for North Miami Beach; Philipp Brutus and Yolly Roberson are state house representatives; and finally, Fred Séraphin is a Miami-Dade County Circuit Court judge. The community fervently hopes that the presence of its elected officials can help shape policies to improve the conditions of all Haitians in Miami-Dade County, including the boat people, in addition to inspiring new generations of Haitian Americans to respond to a call for public service.

Florida State Representative Philipp Brutus speaking
at the January 2002 Haitian Independence Gala in
Boston. Courtesy of the *Boston Haitian Reporter*.

Boston

Although the number of Haitians residing in Boston is not as consequen-
tial as that of New York and Miami, the Bostonian Haitian community is
nonetheless very visible. Government publications place the Haitian population of Boston at approximately 45,000, and they indicate Haiti as the top
country of origin for the foreign-born population. But, it is obvious that the
number is higher, because the same pattern obtains of nonimmigrants who
extend their stay and of immigrants who do not record their presence with
the census. In light of this, one might well accept estimates provided by Haitians themselves to be closer to the reality—that is, about 55,000–60,000 for
the Boston metropolitan statistical area and about 80,000 for the state of
Massachusetts. By all accounts—those of Haitian organizations, and of the

Fred Séraphin, Miami-Dade County Circuit
Court judge. Courtesy of the *Haitian Times.*

Boston Redevelopment Authority in the Mayor's Office—more than 70 percent of the Haitian population reside in the neighborhoods of Mattapan, Dorchester, Hyde Park, and Roxbury, where most Haitian businesses are located. The majority of Haitians in those areas tend to be of working- and lower-middle-class backgrounds, employed primarily in the service industry, as custodians, housekeepers, aides, cooks, and other menial positions of this sort. The remainder of the Haitian population is dispersed in the middle-class neighborhoods of Jamaica Plains, Roslindale, West Roxbury, and the suburbs of Randolph, Milton, and Canton; these Haitians work as professionals in various corporations, institutions, and agencies, both in the private and government sectors.

In many ways, there are some similarities between the Haitian populations of Boston and New York. The Boston Haitian presence dates back to the late 1950s and early 1960s, right after François Duvalier started his reign of terror. While many members of the professional class migrated to New York, a few others came to Boston in search of educational opportunities. An article about Haitians in Boston published in the October 2001 issue of the *Boston Haitian Reporter* traces the origin "of the first stirrings of a growing community" in 1965–1970. According to Gerdès Fleurant from Wellesley College's Department of Music, quoted in the article, the Haitian community lived primarily in Mattapan, Dorchester, and the fringes of Roxbury. At the time, the community was small, consisting of about 100 people belonging to 20 families. Fleurant was a member of the early Haitian community, which at the time was composed, he said, of "students, professionals or academics." The article goes on to say that the influx of educated Haitians in Boston continued in the 1970s, as many Haitians who had originally gone to Africa—to Congo, in particular—at a time when many African nations, having won their independence and wanting to liberate themselves from the Europeans, turned to Haiti for their professional cadre. Several members of this group of Haitians chose to leave Africa and to relocate to Boston, known as a "hotbed of education and academic activity," while others went to New York and Chicago. In time, these Haitians continued to send for their relatives still in Haiti, and eventually the community grew larger and larger. Not all members of the growing Haitian community had a Haitian university education to begin with and were as lucky as Fleurant, who himself remarks: "while a few Haitians came to Boston to find the welcome of relatives who own homes, most were renters and struggled to find jobs and affordable housing.... Most worked menials jobs as cooks or dishwashers in restaurants or in college dining facilities. Many went without regular medical care." The same October 2001 issue of the *Boston Haitian Reporter* had another article about another pioneer of the Boston Haitian community, Jacques Borges, who is referred to as the "the Godfather of the Boston community." Borges's recollection of the early days revealed the closeness of these Haitian families, who kept Haitian traditions alive. These included the "traditional Sunday pumpkin soup...and popular Haitian games such as dominoes and besig [a card game]." These gatherings also provided "a forum to evoke the good old days in Haiti and the most current news." These traditions are still firmly ingrained in all the Haitian communities throughout the United States.

Today's Bostonian Haitians have formed a vibrant community where the entrepreneurial and community spirit is as strong as ever. Mattapan is the Boston neighborhood where the largest number of Haitians (particularly the newcomers) reside. As one Haitian interviewed in the context of fieldwork describes, "Mattapan is the heart of the Haitian community," and more than any other neighborhood in the city, this is where one has the greatest chance of finding "things Haitian"—such as food; beauty supplies; records, cassettes, CDs, and videos; newspapers; Vodou artifacts; artwork; and the like—all on the same street. Indeed, Haitian businesses—bakeries, restaurants, music shops, conve-nience stores, retail stores, money transfer companies, computer and fax cen-ters—are prominent in Mattapan's major commercial streets, River and Blue Hill avenues. Prominently displayed are signs such as *Le Foyer, Bon Appétit, Picasso, Chez Nanou, CAM Caribbean, Bobby Express,* that suggest Haitian ownership. The farmer's market at the intersection of River Street and Cum-mins Highway carries Haitian produce, and is well-known to Bostonian Hai-tians, some of them coming from other neighborhoods on shopping excursions. Animated conversations in Haitian Creole can be heard as the passerby or the fieldworker strolls along these sidewalks or waits for the train or the bus at Mattapan Square, where billboards advertising health care, for example, are also written in Haitian Creole. A couple of Haitian doctors and lawyers have also established their clinics and offices in the neighborhood, in order to better assist their Haitian clientele; others have their practices in Dorchester, Hyde Park, and Roxbury. Haitians of the Catholic faith attend services in Haitian Creole at St. Angela Church located on Blue Hill Avenue in Mattapan or at St. Matthews in Dorchester. Likewise, Protestants, Baptists and Adventists do not have far to go to worship as a host of churches are found all over the neighborhood, such as the First Haitian Baptist Church (Mattapan), New Pentecostal Church of God (Mattapan), Dorchester Church of the Nazarene, Haitian Church of God of Boston, and Église de Dieu (Dorchester). The same applies to Vodou practitioners who have their needs met by *oungans* and *manbos* throughout the community.

The Haitian community of Boston has a great deal of media outlets that focus on Haitian and Haitian American matters. The *Boston Haitian Reporter* is a well respected monthly newspaper that, in addition to reporting news of concern about the Haitian community both in Boston and the United States, has quite a number of educational columns well written and well researched, among them articles on the Louisiana Purchase, Toussaint Louverture, the U.S. occupation of Haiti, and Jean-Baptiste Pointe DuSable (the Black man from Saint-Domingue origin who founded the city of Chicago). The histori-cal dimension of this newspaper makes it a very valuable source of informa-tion. The level of visibility that this newspaper commands is evident in the number of both Haitians and non-Haitians who choose to advertise their businesses in the paper. Moreover, the Mayor's Office of the New Bostonians has a publication, *New Bostonians Guide to City Services,* that is available in Haitian Creole, *Nouvo Bostonians Gid pou Sèvis Vil la.* These facts convinc-ingly attest to the visibility of the Haitian community in Boston. In addition to print media, there are several low frequency radio stations that operate on a 24-hour basis. Radio Concorde, Radio Nouveauté, Radio Soleil, and

Radio Energie, are the most popular ones. In addition, many other radio programs both on FM and AM offer a variety of programming ranging from news, *konpa* music, art, and religion. In fact, the same October 2001 issue of the *Haitian Boston Reporter* mentioned earlier lists some thirty or so Haitian radio programs. Haitian television programs exist on Tele Kreyòl station and HAIENET TV, in addition to others on cable TV, such WCEA TV/Channel 19, ABCI, *Camera Mosaique, Tele Diaspora,* and *Tele Energie.*

In Boston, one can also find quite numerous Haitian community-based organizations and centers, involved in matters of legal and immigration advocacy, economic development, housing assistance, health education, domestic violence, and other social service issues. Some of the better known include the Asosyasyon Fanm Ayisyen nan Boston (AFAB; Association of Haitian Women in Boston), the Haitian American Public Health Initiative (HAPHI), the Haitian Multi-Service Center (under the auspices of the Boston Catholic Charities), the Center for Community Health Education and Research (CCHER), the Haitian-Americans United, Inc. (HAU), and the Haitian Coalition of Somerville. In fact, these organizations joined together to organize peaceful demonstrations in front of the INS office (located in the John F. Kennedy Federal Building) to protest the detention of Haitian refugees in Florida (as can be recalled from chapter 4). The Haitian-Americans United Association is also well known for taking the leadership to organize the various activities associated with Haitian Heritage Month, including the Haitian American Unity Parade held in the month of May, as well as the Haitian Independence Gala in January (chapter 2). In the same connection can be mentioned the Association of Haitian Artists of New England (based in Boston), and the Cambridge Art Association responsible for putting on various exhibits of Haitian art, as well as promoting the works of Haitian writers and musicians. The Boston public schools, particularly those with large Haitian student populations, are also involved in a variety of cultural enrichment activities, including book fairs, folkloric shows, and the like. These schools include Hyde Park High School, Dorchester High School, Madison Park School (Roxbury), Woodrow Wilson Middle School (Dorchester), Lewemberg Middle School (Mattapan), Kenney Elementary School (Dorchester), and Taylor Elementary School (Mattapan). Some of them have Haitian teachers on their faculty to specifically address the educational needs of Haitian students, among them the newcomers who are enrolled in bilingual education programs. College-age students attend the local colleges and universities, as well as the most prestigious ones of international reputation. In addition, a couple of Haitian professors are employed at MIT and the University of Massachusetts–Boston, among other institutions of higher education throughout the state of Massachusetts. In the same vein, the University of Massachusetts–Boston's Department of Africana Studies houses the Haitian Studies Association (HSA), founded in 1988. HSA is a national organization composed of scholars from various academic disciplines, whose work focuses on Haiti and the diaspora. HSA is responsible for organizing an annual conference held in the fall on various campuses throughout the country; sometimes the conference is also held in Haiti. HSA also publishes a scholarly journal, the *Journal of Haitian Studies,* produced under the editorship of Dr. Claudine Michel at the University of California–Santa Barbara's Department of Black Studies.

Finally, Bostonian Haitians have had a strong voice in U.S. politics since 1999, when Marie St. Fleur was elected as state house representative from the

Massachusetts State Representative Marie St. Fleur speaking on the steps of the State House. Also pictured is gubernatorial candidate Scott Harshbarger. Courtesy of the *Boston Haitian Reporter.*

Fifth Suffolk District, representing Dorchester and part of Roxbury. Haitians are exceptionally proud of Marie St. Fleur, who is the first Haitian American ever to hold elected office in the state of Massachusetts. The "girl from the neighborhood" (as her campaign slogan reads) is the pride of the entire Haitian diaspora, and she is a sought-after speaker who is often seen at the forefront of Haitian demonstrations to fight for the fair treatment of Haitian refugees. St. Fleur is certainly one of the most-respected members of the Haitian American community.

Chicago

Haitian immigrants have also settled in the Midwest; Chicago is the city where the majority of these Haitian Midwesterners are located. Estimates of the population range from 5,000 to 15,000 for the Chicago metropolitan statistical area, and from 15,000 to 30,000 for the state of Illinois. The smaller size of the Chicago Haitian community makes it less visible than those of New York, Miami, and Boston, in the sense that Chicago does not have easily recognizable Haitian neighborhoods comparable to those of Brooklyn, Little Haiti, Mattapan, or Dorchester. Haitians tend to be widely dispersed in and about Chicago, and they also reside in the adjacent cities of Evanston and Skokie, and in the West suburbs. However, Haitians in the Chicago area represent the whole gamut of social classes ranging from professionals with well-paid jobs in the government and private sectors to middle- and working-class individuals employed in various agencies and industries throughout the cities to poor undocumented entrants working at low-paid menial jobs, who migrated north after an initial stay in Florida to join relatives.

They too have formed their own community-based and professional organizations to serve the needs of the community. Additionally, they have their popular diasporic media that broadcast Haitian and Haitian American affairs. The better known of Haitian community centers in the Chicago area is the Haitian American Community Association (HACA), which maintains two offices, one on Chicago's North Side and the other in Evanston. This center was created some twenty-five years ago to provide social services to low-income and working-class Haitians. It focuses on HIV prevention and education; immigration and translation assistance; housing referrals and advocacy; and emergency food, shelter, and clothing assistance. Recently, HACA has taken the leadership to organize a well attended social event, an annual Haitian picnic, held on the 4th of July in a park in Evanston, intended to bring the Haitian community together. Other organizations include the Haitian American Immigrants Association (HAIA); Operation SOS which raises money for people who have AIDS in Haiti; the Concerned Haitian Americans of Illinois (CHAI) located in Rockford, Illinois, which sponsors an annual fund-raising dinner for a variety of social programs; and the Haitian Heritage Council. The Haitian Catholic Mission at Our Lady of Peace Parish on the South Side also sponsors various community-oriented programs and attends to the needs of the Haitian Catholic community. In addition, Our Lady of Peace Church conducts masses in Haitian Creole on Sundays; other parishioners go to St. Jerome and St. Mary's in Evanston. There are also many Protestant churches, among them the First Haitian Baptist Church of Evanston, l'Église Haïtienne Missionnaire du Nord, l'Église Haïtienne d'E-vanston, and l'Église Haïtienne de la Grâce. Moreover, there exist in the Chicago area some Haitian-owned businesses, such as the Ascar Travel Agency, whose owner is also the executive director of Operation SOS, Soleil Enterprises, and La Gonave Economic Development. Caribana, Rendez-vous, and Le Creole are three Haitian restaurants well-known to the community. With regard to Haitian diasporic media in Chicago, one can mention three popular radio programs: *Radio L'union,* connected with Loyola University of Chicago, which focuses mostly on political news, in addition to community matters; *Radio Men Kontre,* which deals with political news and community happenings on Sundays; and *Vwa Lakay,* which plays *konpa* music on Saturdays. In addition, there are a couple of television programs that are widely viewed. These include *Azaka-Bellade TV,* available on channel 21 in Chicago, and on channel 6 in Evanston; *Unity in Diversity, Zaboka,* and *Haiti Jeunesse,* which air on public or community access channels.

In addition to maintaining these Haitian-specific outlets, the Haitian community also participates in a number of Caribbean- and Black-organized activities, such as *Carifèt* held in August, and the African Art Festival held on the Labor Day weekend. In fact, the latter event—whose organizing committee included Harry Fouché, then host of the popular *Radio L'Union*—brought in 2002 a well-known Haitian artist, Emeline Michel, who performed in front of a diverse crowd of Chicagoans and visitors. Further, the Haitian professional community of Chicago is involved in the mainstream affairs of the city and has achieved some level of visibility and recognition. One example of such involvement is the Haitian participation in the DuSable Park Coalition. The City of Chicago is committed to recognizing the contribution of Jean-Baptiste Pointe DuSable, the Black Saint-Domingan to whom the early beginnings of Chicago's development is attributed, and has dedicated commemorative parkland in his honor on the waterfront where the Chicago River meets Lake Michigan. The DuSable Park Coalition includes the well-known Chicago Chapter of the Association of Haitian Physicians Abroad and the Midwest

Association of Haitian Women. The goals of this coalition are to oversee the development of the DuSable Park, intended to educate Chicagoans and visitors around the United States and the world about the origin of Chicago and to provide a public space for a variety of recreational and cultural activities. Additionally, Haitians are also working with the DuSable League, another city organization, interested in "the preservation and dissemination of the history and culture of Chicago's first permanent non-native-American settler, Jean Baptiste Pointe DuSable, a Black man who built his home around 1772 on the north bank of the Chicago River."[7] Moreover, Haitians have begun making some strides in politics, as one of their own, Lionel Jean-Baptiste, is an alderman in Evanston's city council. All these facts convincingly attest to the Haitian visibility of the Chicago area. In the words of Harry Fouché, former host of *Radio L'Union* who headed the Haitian Consulate in New York City from May 2003 to April 2004, "being a smaller community, there are many things you would not have expected to happen here that have."[8] Indeed, since its origin, Haitians have always been part of the fabric of the city of Chicago; there is no doubt that they will continue to leave their indelible mark on the Midwest metropolis.

THINGS HAITIAN

The panoramic profile of Haitian life in selected American cities enables us to see that Haitians constitute a very visible segment of American society. The Haitian community has come together to inscribe its history, culture, and perspectives into the collective American experience, thus contributing to the formation of a "new" America. Indeed, a significant number of things Haitian are becoming part of the American landscape. Among them can be recalled: (1) Toussaint Louverture Elementary School in Miami, named after the Haitian revolutionary hero; (2) Avenue Morisseau-Leroy in the Edison/Little River area of Miami known as Little Haiti, renamed to honor the Haitian poet; (3) Little Haiti's 54th Street renamed Boulevard Toussaint Louverture; (4) Haitian voices in American politics as seen primarily in Miami and Boston; and (5) the Haitian Heritage Month in May, where various events take place throughout major American cities, all receiving extensive media coverage. For example, in New York, Governor Pataki recognized the date of May 18, 2003, as the 200th anniversary of Haitian Flag Day. Also, on May 12, 2003, the Empire State Building was illuminated with red and blue lights to commemorate the Haitian Flag. On May 23, 2003, at the famous Carnegie Hall in New York City, a theatrical performance, "Haiti: The Rhythms, the Dances and the Gods," was staged by Mapou Productions in association with the

Haitian Musical Heritage Foundation to recognize Haitian history. African American Danny Glover, longtime defender of Haitians, played the revolutionary hero Toussaint Louverture before a "sold out enthusiastic crowd."[9] Moreover, various parades and music festivals, such as the Haitian Unity Parade in Boston, or the *Konpa* festival in Miami contribute to the recognition of the Haitian presence in the United States.

Of all the activities organized by the Haitian community, its musical festivals are the ones that attract the largest audiences composed of both Haitians and non-Haitians and perhaps receive the highest visibility. The *Konpa* festival that celebrated its fifth anniversary in 2003 is an event to which Miami residents have grown accustomed. Moreover, the large tourist population of Miami attends this joyous occasion as well. Centrally staged in Bayfront Park, this major music festival takes place annually in the month of May, in conjunction with the festivities of Haitian Flag Day. This is where some 20,000 fans, listeners, and bystanders get to experience firsthand the power of Haitian *mizik rasin* (as was defined in chapter 3), embedded in such popular artists and groups as Wyclef Jean, Beethova Obas, Emeline Michel, Farah Juste, Tabou Combo, Sweet Micky, Konpa Kreyòl, T-Vice, Djakout Mizik, Boukman Eksperyans, Carimi, Nu Look, D-Zine, and many others. Some describe this festival as one of the most celebrated ethnic events in Miami and say that visitors from all continents come to dance to the boisterous rhythms of Haitian drums. Haitians owe the success of this festival to the popularity of Haitian music and the impact of Haitian artists who have achieved international recognition. One such artist is undoubtedly Wyclef Jean, who made his debut with a group called the Fugees—a name that is short for the word *refugees,* chosen at a time when Haitian refugees were stacked up in Guantanamo Bay (Cuba) by the INS. In 1997, Wyclef Jean released his first solo album, *The Carnival,* which instantly made him an American and perhaps a world icon. Smaller versions of the *Konpa* festival occur in other cities, for example the *Kreyolfest* that took place in June 2003 at Wingate Park in Brooklyn, New York. Haitian music is perhaps one of the strongest unifying factors among Haitians. As further evidence of this, one can mention the Haitian Music Entertainment Awards (in its sixth year at the time of this writing), established to celebrate the achievements of Haitian and Haitian American artists. This event is also attended by leading African American artists.

In addition to the various Haitian and Haitian American organizations already mentioned in our description of selected cities, there is another well-respected national organization called the National Organization for the Advancement of Haitians (NOAH) based in Washington, D.C. NOAH was founded in 1991 as a nonprofit social policy corporation, originally in

Haitian American hip-hop artist Wyclef Jean attending
the 2003 Flag Celebration in New York, along with a
young fan. Courtesy of the *Haitian Times*.

response to the Haitian refugee crisis. This organization has chapters in
Miami, New York, Chicago, Atlanta, Los Angeles, and Port-au-Prince. "[It] is
recognized as a public policy information clearinghouse and advocate for the
democratization of Haiti and is consulted by the executive branch of the
United States as an intermediary between the governmental and private sectors within Haiti and abroad."[10] Every year NOAH organizes an annual
awards gala to honor outstanding Haitian Americans. Former honorees
include Fred Séraphin, Miami-Dade County Circuit Court judge; Jacques
Despinosse, councilman for the city of North Miami; Dr. Rudolph Moise,
owner of the Comprehensive Health Center and of the Haitian Radio Carnivale in Miami, and Marie St. Fleur, Massachusetts state house representative
from Boston, names that the reader can recall from our earlier discussion. Furthermore, in other cities where enclaves of Haitians are found, namely Newark

(New Jersey), Philadelphia, St. Louis, and Atlanta, they have also formed their own associations and have other diasporic publications, for example *Le* Club Haïtien de St. Louis, or the Association for Haitian American Development (AHAD) in Atlanta, which publishes a journal called *Creole Connection.* In fact, the Haitian population of Altanta is on the rise, as reported in a recent article published in the *Haitian Times* (December 10–16, 2003, pp. 12–13) that estimates the size of the Haitian community in Metro Atlanta at 4,415 people. Similarly, there is a growing Haitian community on the West Coast, mostly in California, where Haitians have formed the Bay Area Haitian American Community Organization (BAHACO), headed by well-known Haitian activist Max Blanchet, who is the president of the FONKOZE USA Foundation (Foundation Kole Zepòl, the Shoulder-to-Shoulder Foundation). Founded in 1997, this foundation is an alternative bank for Haiti's poor, which provides the financial and educational services they need to empower themselves and their communities. Moreover, in addition to the Haitian Studies Association (discussed earlier in the Boston section), there exists another academic organization, KOSANBA, or the Congress of Santa Barbara, which was created in 1997 by a group of leading Haitian academics from well-known universities for the scholarly study of Haitian Vodou. KOSANBA is housed in the Center for Black Studies at the University of California at Santa Barbara, and it organizes an annual conference, sometimes held in conjunction with the HSA's meetings. On the topic of Haitian Vodou as an academic discipline, one can also mention that in November 1997 Spelman College in Atlanta in the context of the Haitian Culture Awareness Week hosted a conference titled Vodoo Demystified. These events organized by Haitian scholars of the diaspora enable members of the Haitian immigrant community to bring Haitian traditions to the fore of U.S. academic discourse.

It is obvious that Haitian immigrants in the United States are determined to change the negative image that some may have about Haitians and their traditions. Furthermore, they are determined to make progress and to prosper in this land of opportunity. They do not want to be left behind. Their intent is well reflected in the latest actions of the National Coalition for Haitian Rights. Indeed, NCHR, under the leadership of former executive director Dina Paul-Parks, drafted a national Haitian American agenda, intended to help Haitians empower themselves, and be a collective force to be reckoned with. To this end, it organized in Miami in April 2002 its first national conference, choosing as its theme "Developing a National Haitian-American Agenda: Moving Forward Together." The conference brought together well-respected Haitian Americans from around the country. These comprised individuals whose names are now familiar, for example: Mayor Josaphat Celestin from North

Miami; Florida State House Representative Philipp Brutus; Massachusetts State House Representative Marie St. Fleur; Dr. Jacques Jiha, then deputy comptroller for New York City (now for New York State); Dr Rudolph Moise from the Comprehensive Health Center of Miami; Gepsie Metellus, executive director of the Haitian Neighborhood Center in Miami (mentioned in chapter 4); and Harry Fouché, former host of *Radio L'Union* in Chicago, who currently works as a senior research economist for the state of Illinois following a short tenure as consul general of the Haitian Consulate in New York. Representatives from leading Haitian American media outlets and organizations described earlier were also present. These included the editors of the *Haitian Times* and of the *Boston Haitian Reporter,* members of the Haitian Studies Association board of directors and advisory committee, as well as several other prominent individuals representing the educational, health, journalistic, legal, and business sectors, in addition to academia. The conference also featured American speakers (both White and Black), who have always been strong advocates of the Haitian cause or whose agencies have always helped Haitians.

Panelists speaking at the National Coalition for Haitian Rights Meeting in April 2002 in Miami. Sitting at the table are Harry Fouché, former host of *Radio L'Union* in Chicago and former Consul General of the Haitian Consulate in New York, and Alix Cantave, founding president of the Haitian Studies Association. Courtesy of the *Haitian Times.*

In short, these various things Haitian, several involving state and local government elected officials, some involving grassroots activists and others involving academics, are intended to remind Americans of the ethnic diversity of America and to foster a knowledge and understanding of the various groups of people (old and new) who constitute the American mosaic. Their existence brings validity to the notion that the United States is "a nation of peoples."

NOTES

1. Some of the New York information is taken from Zéphir's earlier works (1996 and 2001). Updated information was, however, obtained through conversations with community members and through media reports.

2. Brown (2001).

3. Concerning the origin of the name *Little Haiti,* there is an interesting anecdote that was told to me (in the context of fieldwork) by the owner of the oldest Haitian store in the community, *Les Cousins,* which first opened on August 4, 1973. The owner of the store, Viter Juste, used to write for a small community journal called *Bulletin de la Communauté Haïtienne.* In 1975, he published an article titled "Faisons un Rêve" (Let's Have a Dream), in which he referred to the Edison/Little River area populated by Haitians as "Little Port-au-Prince," modeled after "Little Havana." This article caught the eyes of a reporter from the *Miami Herald,* who wanted to meet with Mr. Juste and find out more about the Haitian community of Miami. Subsequently, the reporter wrote an article about the community for the *Miami Herald* and changed the name "Little Port-au-Prince" to "Little Haiti." This name has been used to refer to this particular Miami neighborhood since the publication of that particular article.

4. Most of the demographic information for Miami-Dade County was obtained from various documents and brochures published by the Edison/Little River Neighborhood Planning Program and the Little Haiti Neighborhood Enhancement Team (NET). Additional information came from other sources, such as grant proposals written by Haitian organizations, in particular the Haitian American Foundation, Inc. (HAFI), headed by Ringo Cayard, and other reports put out by the Immigration and Ethnicity Institute of Florida International University, directed by Dr. Alex Stepick and Dr. Carol Dutton Stepick. These reports are available on the institute's Web site. I am indebted to both Mr. Cayard and Dr. Alex Stepick for making those documents available to me.

5. The term *civic engagement* is taken from Stepick et al. (2002) in their report "Civic Engagement of Haitian Immigrants and Haitian Americans in Miami-Dade County." The report is available on the Florida International University Immigration and Ethnicity Institute's Web site.

6. The information about the Haitian organizations in Miami-Dade County was obtained from a booklet put together by the Society of Haitian-American Professionals and Entrepreneurs (SHAPE) in April 2002. I am indebted to Gepsie Metellus, executive director of the Haitian Neighborhood Center, for making this document available to me.

7. As indicated in the Chicago DuSable League's mission statement, available on its Web site. While doing fieldwork in Chicago in late August 2002, I attended a ceremony, Laying of the Wreath, organized by this league to "memorialize the 184th Anniversary of Jean Baptist

Point DuSable's Life" (as the flyer distributed for the occasion stated), at Pioneer Court on 401 N. Michigan Avenue. At the ceremony, both the invocation and benediction were given by a Haitian priest from the Haitian Catholic Mission of Chicago.

8. As quoted in a *Haitian Times* article titled "Haitian-American Politics in Chicago" (April 10–16, 2002, p. 9).

9. As it has been reported on the following Haitian Web site: http://www.akolad .com/news/Haiti_Rhythms_Dances_gods030523.htm.

10. As quoted from NOAH's Web page.

6

Making It in America: Haitian Immigrants' Ethnic Options

There is little doubt that Haitian immigrants are here to stay. They are determined to make it in America and find successful mechanisms of adjustment and adaptation to their land of resettlement. One such mechanism is to regroup themselves in relatively large ethnic communities that have become very visible and that are contributing to the construction of a new American kaleidoscope, as was discussed in the previous chapter. In their ethnic communities—concentrated mostly in the northeast metropolitan areas of New York City and Boston, in southern Florida (Miami, West Palm Beach, and Fort Lauderdale), and the Greater Chicago area—Haitians have managed to visibly recreate the cultural habits of their homeland. They have established many ethnic businesses and organizations and designed quite a number of ethnic activities in which they prominently display their allegiance to their native country. All these diasporic affairs are important for the preservation of their culture. In their resolve to make it in America, Haitian immigrants make conscious identity choices with regard to who they are and how they want to be perceived by society at large. This chapter explores issues of ethnic identity for the Haitian diaspora, and it demonstrates that Haitian immigrants' notion of ethnicity is shaped, on the one hand, by values directly inherited from the homeland and, on the other, by the realities of the American context. As such, Haitian ethnicity is transnational. The construction of ethnicity is strongly linked to the immigration experience, which, in the first place, has engendered the concept of *diaspora,* and which, subsequently, forces an immigrant to develop new mechanisms for survival, acceptance, and ultimately success in the host society.

In the discussion of identity formation among Haitian immigrants, it is necessary to make a distinction between first and second generation, as trends in ethnic identification are not identical for both groups. Generally speaking, the operational definition used by most sociologists is that the first generation consists of the "immigrants or the foreign-born population"; the second of the "sons and daughters of the first generation"; and the third of the "sons and daughters of the second generation."[1] As was discussed in previous chapters, the Haitian immigrant population of the United States (legal and illegal) is estimated at close to one million. By looking at INS records, inferences can be made with regard to the approximate size of both generations. The newness of the Haitian diaspora (unlike the European diaspora), whose steady and uninterrupted migration really began in the early 1960s when François Duvalier became president of the country, explains why the third generation has not yet come of age to constitute a significant entity to be studied separately. In this discussion, the small percentage of the third generation that exists is subsumed under the broader category of second generation, since members of that generation are also the sons and daughters of the foreign-born generation. As can be recalled from chapter 4, the Haitian population is relatively young with the majority of approximately 75 percent being under 40 years of age. The second generation comes primarily from that younger population of roughly 750,000 individuals (75% of one million). Within that group, most members of the second generation are under 30 years of age (roughly 70% of 750,000, or 525,000). In short, the second generation comprises at least 525,000 people, and the first 250,000 (25% of a million). In addition to these numbers, both generations share a portion of the population between 30 and 40 years of age. In light of these data, one can safely infer that the first generation is made up of about one-third of the total population of the Haitian diaspora, and the second of the remaining two-thirds. Based on the original estimation of one million people, this translates roughly into 333,333 individuals for the first, and 666,666 for the second, respectively.[2]

DIASPORIC ETHNICITY AND FIRST-GENERATION HAITIAN IMMIGRANTS

In light of their unique historical past and circumstances that transformed them from slaves into a free and independent people, first-generation Haitian immigrants come to the United States with an experiential baggage, which includes a strong sense of who they are and an appreciation for their historical heritage. This experiential baggage fosters the development of a Haitian ethnicity, at the core of which is a sense of racial pride and of belonging to a nation.

Racial Pride and Sense of Belonging to a Nation

Thanks to their unique history, Haitians have developed a nation-based interpretation of the concept of race. It is important to recall that the declaration of independence on January 1, 1804, officially marks the birth of Haiti as a nation and, more important, as the first Black nation ever to liberate itself from the yoke of colonialism and to win its independence. Independent Haiti became the symbol of anticolonialism, African regeneration, and racial equality. The unity of all Blacks (free colored men and slaves alike) against White subjugation is at the root of the establishment of Haiti as a nation. As one scholar remarks, "race was the unifying theme for nationhood."[3] For Haitians, race can be equated with nation because it constituted the basis of their winning and maintaining full autonomy as a republic. In the same connection, other scholars argue that "in their conflation of race and nation all Haitians accept that they are Black and assert that to be Black is to be truly human."[4] In short, the word *Black* for them tends to be synonymous with pride and unflinching independence and has always carried very positive connotations. In addition, Haitians have a definite idea of the importance of Haitian history for the Black world. Regardless of which part of Haiti they come from and the social class occupied in the homeland, they know what their ancestors achieved. Indeed, all throughout the country, they are accustomed to seeing monuments, statues, buildings, and schools dedicated to the memory of their national heroes or built in remembrance of significant events that took place in the course of over five hundred years of Haitian history. Additionally, schooled and educated members of that group learn a great deal about Haitian history in school. They proudly regard themselves as members of the Black race, and boast of the heroic accomplishments of their revolutionary leaders and the international recognition that their writers, intellectuals, and artists have achieved. In discussions of race, Haitians are quick to remind everyone that the blood of Toussaint Louverture and Dessalines flows in their veins and of the significance of 1804—themes that are also found in Haitian and Haitian American diasporic writings, paintings, and songs. Furthermore, as an independent republic of Black people, Haitians do not experience White domination as such. They are the majority; consequently, they are used to self-governance and to seeing Blacks in positions of political, judicial, educational, social, and economic power. These facts contribute to a striking sense of racial pride and of belonging to a nation that is present in most (if not all) members of the first-generation Haitian immigrants, as they arrive in the United States and seek to establish new lives for themselves and their families.[5]

However, while they maintain their sense of belonging to Haiti, they also know the reasons that compel them to relocate to the United States and are aware of the necessity to make it in their New World. Consequently, they are totally determined to make all the necessary sacrifices to ensure the success of their journey and the future of their offspring. However, in spite of this determination, the journey proves perilous, and they face a great many hardships in the course of their resettlement. In the process, they encounter serious obstacles and make difficult choices. One such obstacle is their placement at the bottom of the ladder in American society. In the United States, it is a known fact that race is a fundamental dimension of identification, and it can play an overwhelming role in shaping the life chances of its inhabitants. Haitian immigrants at a very early stage come to realize that they have entered a society that, unlike their own, uses a classification system based on race. Furthermore, they discover that fundamental distinctions exist between the races and that people are still treated differently because of their race. The principle of race equality so deeply ingrained in Haitians' consciousness since 1804 does not necessarily hold true in the United States, particularly in practice. In the United States, the term *Black* does not convey the same positive meaning that it does in the homeland—that is to say freedom, independence, majority, equality, and pride. To some segments of American society, it can mean the exact opposite: inferiority, minority, inequality, and oppression. Haitians know that native Black Americans do encounter racism, discrimination, and segregation in their own country and are endlessly fighting for their civil rights and for social justice. Moreover, they themselves, as a Black group in the United States, have experienced strong instances of discrimination—the most outrageous of these was their classification as AIDS carriers, as well as the Abner Louima case and the differential treatment given to them by INS (see chapter 4). As Black immigrants, they are cognizant of the new label placed on them: "minorities." They also realize that they are subject to the same discriminatory practices as native Blacks and are aware that their assignment to a stigmatized and generic Black classification, with no attention paid to national origin, historical legacy, or cultural traditions, could constitute a serious impediment to their success in the so-called land of opportunity. In fact, it could seriously diminish their chances of securing a better life, thus defeating the very purpose of their immigration. Haitian immigrants are faced with no other choice than to find adaptive strategies to enhance their probability of success in their new place of settlement. One such adaptive strategy is the ethnic option, or ethnicity.

Haitian immigrant ethnicity—of which many manifestations are discussed in chapter 5, including residential distribution, religious practices, music, art, festivals and parades, ethnic organizations and businesses, diasporic media, and celebratory events—thus emerges as a means of survival in a race-defined and racist society. As one scholar notes, Haitian immigrants brandish their ethnicity "in a tactical manner to maintain and protect [their] individual group interests."[6] Therefore, the majority of first-generation Haitian immigrants choose not to become "Americans"—even though some have taken out U.S. citizenship to meet the requirements of some governmental and educational positions as well as those of U.S. immigration to petition for relatives—because becoming Americans can only mean becoming *Black Americans,* whom they realize are placed at the bottom of the totem pole in American society. This placement is in direct conflict with the Haitian definition of Blackness, which is synonymous with pride and unflinching independence. Their race is a symbol of a glorious past, that of the revolution that led to freedom, nationhood, and equality with Whites. Haitians' deep beliefs in the concept of race equality is manifest in their desire to remain Haitians as opposed to becoming Black Americans. This desire is illustrated by their self-identification as Haitians. Indeed, in the context of fieldwork when asked how they choose to refer to themselves in the United States, out of a variety of possible options including African American, American, West Indian, or Caribbean, the overwhelming majority responded *Haitian* (less than 10% chose more than one designation, a point that will be taken up later in the discussion of intergroup relationships). In their minds, the label *Haitian* expresses more the positive meanings of Blackness than does *Black American,* perceived by many first-generation Haitian immigrants to be too stigmatized. In short, first-generation Haitian immigrants want to retain their identity as Haitian. As one Haitian immigrant interviewed during fieldwork puts it, *"l'haïtien sait son chez lui, et il connait ses racines"* (the Haitian has a home that he or she can call his or her own, and he or she knows his or her roots). This statement encapsulates remarkably well the Haitian immigrant's sense of belonging to a nation. This feeling of belonging to a proud tradition explains the sense of self-worth and of purpose that also characterizes Haitian immigrants.

Sense of Self-Worth and of Purpose as Immigrants

"An honest, dignified, and proud people." Those are the words used by a Haitian immigrant to describe his people.[7] Once again, this sense of dignity and pride can be traced as far back as independence, when Haitians considered themselves to be the liberators of the displaced Blacks in the New World.

Moreover, as another Haitian immigrant explains, they feel they can accomplish greatness since they "conquered colonialism." As "conquerors," they believe in themselves and their self-worth and want to contribute to the "Black success story." Many think that it is part of their mission to prove to America that Blacks are not inferior and that Haitians, in particular, are not justly represented by perceptions of poverty, lack of ability, illiteracy, and backwardness. They argue that they "do not have a victim's mentality," but rather "the mentality of a liberated man," to quote another Haitian immigrant. In the words of an elderly Haitian immigrant, "we Haitians, we are *gran moun* [full-fledged individuals] in front of the White man. We are liberated. We have a sense of equality." Presumably, this sense of being *gran moun* transcends the myth and bigotry of racial superiority, and serves as a liberating force that enables them to achieve their goals in the society of resettlement. Moreover, this same sense of self-worth empowers them to want to take control of what they can accomplish in this country and not become fatalists. It is important to keep in mind that, as immigrants, their purpose in coming to the United States is to achieve success and prosperity and not to become failures. Success for the Haitian immigrant can be defined in many ways: It is the story of the Haitian peasant woman pushing an older White Jewish lady in a wheelchair through Central Park (New York) and saving her meager earnings under a mattress to send back home to her children, who otherwise would have nothing. It is the story of the *tap tap* driver (local vans used for public transportation in Haiti) who could not afford the high price of gasoline resulting from the U.S. embargo on Haiti and who now owns a "gypsy" cab in Brooklyn. It is the story of the woman who was laid off when the American-owned baseball factory in Port-au-Prince closed down and was no longer bringing home a two-dollar-a-day wage and who now cleans luxurious hotel rooms in South Beach or Fort Lauderdale. It is the story of the baker who now owns a Creole bakery shop in Little Haiti. It is the story of the son of the garbage man and street sweeper who graduated from a prestigious U.S. university and now works on Wall Street. While these stories are not the same, they are all brushstrokes of the same Haitian immigrant portrait. Most important, though, they prove that Haitian immigrants are in this country to improve their conditions, to earn an honest living, and to live with dignity and decency. Therefore, taking any menial job—housekeeping, home attendant, dishwasher, or custodian—is not considered something degrading but rather a means of bringing in some income. For many first-generation Haitian immigrants, economic mobility has nothing to do with the kind of job they do, but rather it is seen in comparison with the situation they had back home. As one Haitian immigrant comments, "the Haitian immigrant has a special attitude. He is ready to make sacrifices. He sees money and his current situation in light of what he left behind." Familiarity with the political and economic situation of Haiti (described in chapter 3) enables us to see why Haitian immigrants are ready to virtually accept all kinds of jobs in the United States, some of the very same ones turned down by Americans (Whites or Blacks). In their search for dignity and hard work, and in order to move themselves out of abject poverty, Haitian immigrants are ready to make many sacrifices, including accepting indignities and exploitation. Many illegal (and unskilled) Haitians in particular claim that they are often paid less than the minimal wage established by law, simply because they have no other option and cannot complain about it to the authorities. It can be mentioned in passing that such conditions hardly lend credence to statements advanced by some conservative sectors of American society that Haitian immigrants are taking jobs away from Americans. For these immigrants, being exploited is part of the tribulations that they must endure on foreign soil in expectation of a better future for their offspring, to whom they relentlessly stress the value of education, considered by them to be the only way out of poverty. In short, first-generation Haitian immigrants are very aware of the conditions of the Haiti they left behind and are mindful of the fact that they are immigrants in the United States. They hope that they will be able to return some day to Haiti and enjoy the hard-won fruits of their labor and sacrifices. The majority of them tend to stress that they have no intention of dying in this country; they are patiently waiting for indications that democracy and political stability are restored and that the economy is recovering. Only time will tell if and when their dream of going back will ever materialize.

Linguistic Identity of First-Generation Haitian Immigrants

Haitian Creole—not French—spoken by all Haitians is the language first-generation Haitian immigrants stress as being their native language. The fact that this particular language is unique to them enables them to maintain their ethnicity and their sense of "peoplehood." Indeed, it is the vernacular language that they use in the context of their daily interactions with members of their family and in their social networks. It is the language that one hears along Flatbush Avenue in Brooklyn, Blue Hill Avenue in Mattapan, and on the *jetneys* (minibuses) of Little Haiti. It is the language used in the various diasporic talk shows and television and radio programs; it is also the language that predominates in Haitian community gatherings and celebrations, such as the various parades and music festivals (see chapter 5). With regard to written Creole, the

major diasporic newspaper, the *Haitian Times,* although written in English, allo-
cates space to a Creole column: "Tèt Ansanm" (Heads Together), written by
Woje E. Saven. This Creole column was first published in the January 5, 2000,
issue. A collection of these selected columns was recently released in a single
volume by the same name (2003). Additionally, one can occasionally find some
Creole advertisements in that paper as well as in the other leading diasporic
paper, the *Boston Haitian Reporter,* which, in March 2004, began printing a
two-page news column in Creole. It is also worth mentioning that a scholarly
journal, the *Journal of Haitian Studies,* published at the University of California–Santa Barbara, accepts contributions in Haitian Creole. In a similar connection, the introduction to the special issue on Haiti published in summer/fall
2002 by *Wadabagei*—a scholarly journal of the Caribbean and its diaspora
housed at Medgar Evers College of the City University of New York—was written in Creole. In sum, in the diasporic context, Haitian Creole emerges as a
marker of Haitian immigrants' ethnolinguistic identity, and it contributes to
their feeling of belonging to a proud cultural and linguistic heritage.

Moreover, all Haitian immigrants agree that Creole is the language that
should be used to address the needs of Haitian immigrants with limited
English proficiency. Indeed, it is a fact that major American cities that are
home to large numbers of Haitian immigrants release some of their publications in Haitian Creole. Those publications pertain to health, education, and
social services. Haitian Creole is also used in all bilingual education programs
that cater to newly arrived Haitian students and is learned by social service
providers who deal with large segments of Haitian immigrants, be they teachers, lawyers, social workers, nurses, counselors, or psychologists. Consequently,
it is taught in several U.S. universities, including Indiana University–Bloomington, the University of Florida–Gainesville, colleges of the City University
of New York, and the University of Massachusetts–Boston, among others. In
addition, there is a telecommunication network called Language Line Services—previously owned by AT&T—which provides interpretation services
in Haitian Creole (along with other foreign languages) to a variety of businesses, including hospitals and clinics, banks, telephone companies, police
departments, district attorney offices, and many other private or government
agencies. These facts clearly demonstrate that Haitian Creole is the recognized language of the Haitian community.

Although Haitian Creole is the shared language of all Haitians, since it is
spoken by the entire population of Haiti, and is an ethnic marker for the Haitian diasporic community, it is, nevertheless, important to acknowledge the
existence of a small percentage of the population that is, in addition, French
speaking. For bilingual Haitians, including those of the diaspora, French still

maintains a social function. In the United States, bilingual speakers do realize that Americans tend to have a fascination for the French language and things French, which they consider chic and classy. Therefore, some play on this fascination and stress their French-speaking ability and their francophone heritage, in the hope that these positive characteristics can be extended to them as well. They sometimes use the French language and the French aspect of their culture (vestiges of French colonialism) as a means of gaining status and obtaining favorable treatment particularly from Whites, which could include job preference over other Blacks. It appears that these particular bilinguals use French as a tool that they hope can enable them to receive an improved placement on the social ladder in American society. In fact, some argue that their knowledge of French should allow them to be counted among the *francophones d'Amérique* (French speakers of America), which is a classification perceived by them to be much more desirable than that of the *minorités d'Amérique* (America's minorities).[8]

Within the Haitian diaspora community, there have long been in existence several periodicals that are written in French, *Haïti en Marche* (Marching Haiti), *Haïti Progrès* (Haiti in Progress), and *Haïti Observateur* (the Haitian Observer), all claiming a French readership among the bilingual diaspora. In the same vein, it is interesting to note that a couple of years ago the leading Haitian American weekly newspaper, the *Haitian Times,* started publishing a French column called *Du côté de chez Hugues* (Hughes's corner). The inaugural column appeared in the January 30–February 5, 2002, issue. Moreover, very recently, a new Haitian magazine written in French, *Haïtiens Aujourd'hui* (Today's Haitians) was launched out of Miami. Its editor-in-chief calls it the first international magazine *"qui honore les Haïtiens"* (that honors Haitians). This magazine is intended to portray Haiti in a positive light (as opposed to the negative images displayed, particularly in the media) and to establish a link with other Haitian diasporic communities living in Montreal and in France as well as with the rest of the francophone world. In this discussion, it is useful to mention that bilingual Haitian immigrants were schooled in French, not in Haitian Creole. The introduction of Haitian Creole in the public school system in Haiti occurred in the early 1980s and was, at the time, left to the discretion of particular schools. Therefore, for these bilingual Haitians reading and writing in French comes more naturally than it does in Creole, a language they learned to read at a later stage in their adult life and, in a few cases, cannot read and write at all.

Furthermore, bilingual Haitians certainly take pride in their French literary heritage. Jacques Roumain's *Gouverneurs de la rosée (Masters of the Dew)* and Jean Price-Mars's *Ainsi parla l'oncle (So Spoke the Uncle)* are all classics of francophone literature. In more recent times, Dany Laferrière, who immigrated to Montreal in 1976, rocketed to literary fame with the publication of his first novel *Comment faire l'amour avec un nègre sans se fatiguer* in 1985. This acclaimed novel, immediately translated in English as *How to Make Love to a Negro,* placed Laferrière at the forefront of Quebec literature as well as diasporic literature even here in the United States. Laferrière, who spends a great deal of time in the United States, is one of the most prolific authors of the Haitian diaspora. He writes in French and has carved for himself a privileged place in francophone studies, owing to the publication of a dozen novels (most of which have also been translated into English). Laferrière's visibility was well captured in the January 2003 French column of the *Haitian Times,* which referred to him as "Le phénomène Dany Laferrière" (the Dany Laferrière phenomenon) and devoted a series of three essays to him. Additionally, one can mention that another Haitian writer, Lilas Desquiron, thanks to her novel *Les chemins de Loco-Miroir* (whose English translation, *Reflections of Loko Miwa,* appeared shortly after), also joined the ranks of the literary diaspora that targets an international readership. The use of the French language gives an international dimension to the works of these and other authors and unquestionably enriches the francophone literary canon. Additionally, they offer valuable insights into Haitian culture, not always accurately represented abroad. The literary channel is perhaps the strongest vehicle that allows Haitian immigrants to maintain a link with the francophone world. Those who appreciate this tradition are not ready to relinquish it and want to preserve it, as they associate with it a number of social benefits that fit into their goals of making a better life and improving their status. This explains why some Haitian bilinguals also choose to claim a broader francophone identity and welcome membership into the francophone world as well.

Intergroup Relationships

Through their attachment to their homeland or nation, their language, their religion, and their particular lifestyle, Haitian immigrants have managed to remain a separate Black ethnic group in the United States. Haitians define their Blackness in terms of linguistic, cultural, and religious traditions directly inherited from Africa, which constitute a source of pride that enables them to sustain the harshness of racism in the United States, where Blackness does not carry the positive connotations that it does in the homeland.

Their desire not to be perceived as an inferior group, but as a group capable of high achievements frequently manifests itself in a certain distancing from other groups occupying the same subordinate position, particularly from native Black Americans. As has been pointed out by another scholar, "Haitians tend to develop forms of identity with a marked pattern toward disaffiliation from the black American population." The same scholar goes on to explain how this disaffiliation sometimes surfaces in the common saying among Haitians, "I don't want to be Black twice."[9] Therefore, many first-generation Haitian immigrants in the context of their everyday lives exploit to a great extent the various aspects of their identity that make them distinct from African Americans, or any other group, for that matter. Their desire to remain a distinct group explains why common Haitian folks prefer to remain within the circle of their Haitian compatriots, and participate only in Haitian affairs. However, one needs to realize that this distancing from African Americans neither means a rejection of Blackness nor the absence of racial consciousness on their part. Their sense of Blackness "is linked to Haitian history through Africa and not to the black experience in the United States."[10]

Moreover, it needs to be stressed that the tendency to distance oneself from other groups is more prevalent among the common folks than among Haitian professionals and leaders of organizations. There exists a fair number of Haitians who find that this tactic does not necessarily guarantee better treatment or placement on the American social ladder. Repeated instances of discrimination on the part of some members of American society, who perceive Haitians to be AIDS carriers and a source of problems for the society in general, lead many Haitians to rethink their perspectives on the reality of race relations in the United States and to discard some of their pretensions to superiority over other Blacks. This manifests itself in the need to recognize the commonalities of a pan-Caribbean and pan-African experience and to join forces with outside communities, as opposed to remaining solely within the confines of the Haitian diasporic community.

On one level, the reality is such that it is not entirely unusual to find a small percentage of Haitians who consider themselves also as West Indians, Caribbeans, or islanders (in addition, of course, to Haitians). Moreover, Haitians, who are fluent speakers of Spanish and who phenotypically can pass as Hispanics, sometimes opt to claim a Hispanic identity (mostly Dominican). These various classifications make some sense when one keeps in mind that a significant number of Haitians live in neighborhoods populated by West Indians and other Spanish Caribbean groups. In New York City, for example, Jamaicans and Dominicans are the largest Caribbean groups. The same situation obtains in Miami, which also has a very large Caribbean population. Therefore, Haitians, for whom the label *Haitian* is as stigmatized as the label *African American,* can regroup themselves under a pan-Caribbean identity and culture, which include some common characteristics—music, food, lifestyle—shared by all the islands. In this perspective, one can mention Haitians' involvement in the West Indian American Day Carnival held on Brooklyn's Eastern Parkway on Labor Day, and the *Carifêt* Festival and the African Art Festival that take place in Chicago during the summer. Such events suggest that there is a growing recognition on the part of Haitian professionals that complete ethnic separateness and attitudes of disdain toward other Black groups are not the best ways to improve the social conditions of Haitians in the United States. The underlying message is that it is quite possible for Haitians to be proud of their ethnic heritage without segregating themselves from other Black groups, who by virtue of their Blackness share similar experiences of discrimination and have common objectives. In fact, several Haitians acknowledge the benefits of membership in this broader geographical category and find some advantages in affiliating with other Black immigrant groups who, like them, are trying to come to grips with the reality of race and ethnic relations in the host society.

Yet on another level, while it is true that the general populace of first-generation Haitian immigrants do not manifest tangible manifestations of identification with native Black Americans, the same cannot be said for Haitians occupying leadership positions, in a variety of fields ranging from government, politics, business, medicine, academia, journalism, to the entertainment industry. As evidence of this, one can witness the high level of interactions between Haitian American and African American leaders in their struggle for racial equality. When it comes to fighting for Haitian rights, Haitian American leaders have always sought the support of Black Americans, many of whom have steadfastly stood by Haitians. A case in point is the involvement of the Congressional Black Caucus and the NAACP in the matter of the Haitian boat people, discussed in chapter 4. In addition, at the time of this writing, some members of the African American community, under the leadership of actor Danny Glover and of Dr. Ron Daniels—founder and chairman of the Haiti Support Project, who had worked with Jesse Jackson's National Rainbow Coalition and who was on the Executive Council of the National Organizing Committee for the historic Million Man March held in 1995—were working together with both Haitian American and African American organization leaders to organize a cruise to commemorate the Haitian Bicentennial in 2004. The *Cruising into History* ship was slated to depart from Miami and to arrive in Haiti on August 14, 2004. As the trip organizers explained, the date of August 14 was purposely chosen to coincide with the historic ceremony of Bois-Caïman held by slave Boukman to set the final details for the massive slave revolution that began in 1791 and led to Haitian independence on January 1, 1804 (see chapter 2).[11]

Ambassador-at-large for war crimes, Pierre-Richard Prosper, at his swearing-in ceremony in Washington, D.C., on July 13, 2002. Also pictured are his proud parents, and Secretary of State Colin Powell. Courtesy of the *Boston Haitian Reporter*.

SECOND-GENERATION HAITIAN IMMIGRANTS

This group is certainly more numerous and more heterogeneous than the first generation.[12] Generally speaking, it is understood that the greater number of children of Haitian immigrants tend to fall within two broad classifications: (1) those who were born here in the United States, who have always lived in this country and may or may not have had a chance to visit Haiti; and (2) those born in Haiti who came to the United States at an early age (usually before adolescence) and are schooled in this country, and who may not have spent any time or significant amount of time in Haiti since their relocation. For members of both categories, the United States is undoubtedly the most familiar environment. Additionally, they are fluent in English, a language that they speak with no accent; some may also have an active or passive knowledge of Haitian Creole (French in rare instances). However, there are other cases that do not neatly fit into the aforementioned classifications. One such case consists of an entire cohort of children of Haitian immigrants, who were born in the United States but were raised in Haiti until they completed their primary education and, in some cases, part of their secondary education. Parents' dissatisfaction with the public schools in the inner cities where many reside, coupled with the problem of child care, explain their choice to have their children schooled in Haiti. Usually they send for them toward their last years of high school, in order to establish a U.S. school record that makes the college admission process easier. These children come regularly to visit their parents in the United States during the summer months. Another group includes children born and raised in Haiti for similar reasons but who, generally, have been spending most of their vacation time with their parents, who migrated earlier to the United States. For those two groups of children, Haiti is the most familiar environment. They possess a native command of Haitian Creole and also have varying degrees of competency in English as a result of repeated sojourns in the United States. Finally, the second generation comprise a very small number of children who either left Haiti at an earlier age and migrated to, or were born in, another location—Montreal, Latin America, other Caribbean islands, or France—before settling with or joining their parents in the United States. In short, the second generation of Haitian immigrants, by its very composition, is more diversified than the first.

Nevertheless, in spite of its heterogeneous composition, the majority of the second generation, with the exception of the newcomers, do not speak English with an accent (or the same heavy accent as the parents) and have a great deal of familiarity with the American way. Because of these characteristics, they are certainly not overtly distinguishable from American Blacks. In consequence, second-generation Haitian immigrants seem to have more ethnic options at their disposal than do the parents. To a large extent, they exhibit variations with regard to their identity choices, their perceptions of, and opinions about, issues of race and ethnicity in the United States. In many ways, they are similar to other second-generation Black immigrants, who have received scholarly attention, as they show the same patterns of ethnic identification, ranging from an identification as Americans (to be understood as Black Americans for obvious reasons), an identification as "ethnic" Americans, to an identification as immigrants "in a way that does not reckon with American racial and ethnic categories."[13] For the purpose of this discussion, second-generation Haitians can be grouped in three broad categories: (1) those who display a strong form of Haitianness; (2) those who display a weaker form of Haitianness; and (3) those who have absolutely nothing to do with Haiti, the undercovers.

Strong Form of Haitianness

In its stronger form, Haitianness is demonstrated mostly through an intense involvement in the Haitian diasporic community and an interest in

Haitian matters at home and in the United States. It can also be expressed by a preference for the label *Haitian* as a self ethnic descriptor, an acknowledgment of one's birthplace of Haiti and parents' birthplace, length of residency in Haiti or repeated trips to Haiti, and a high level of fluency in Haitian Creole.

Generally speaking, individuals who display a stronger form of Haitianness think that there is no label other than *Haitian* that could describe them adequately and want to be known as such, because they were born and had lived in Haiti for some time. Moreover, they have completed a significant amount of their education in Haiti. They speak Creole without much English interference and feel very knowledgeable about Haiti. They have familiarity with the current political situation, know the history, and venerate cultural heroes. These individuals also feel it is their duty to educate Haitian American youth who have always lived in the United States (as well as others) about the cultural richness of Haiti, as a way to counteract the negative images presented in the media. Those who are still in high school or in college are very active in Haitian clubs and organizations and volunteer their time in many community activities. Those who are already gainfully employed remain connected to the Haitian community and are members of the various Haitian diasporic organizations and associations mentioned in chapter 5. Additionally, they maintain a very close relationship with their parents with whom they share similar values, such as the importance of education, a sense of self-worth, and a sense of racial pride and of belonging to a nation. Whatever their occupation, they have a strong commitment to the Haitian community and want to make a contribution to the Haitian cause, here in the United States or at home. Prominent members of the second generation who arguably might be illustrative of a stronger form of Haitianness owing to their commitment to Haitian affairs include, for example, writer Edwidge Danticat, artist Wyclef Jean, artist Lolo Beaubrun of the *mizik rasin* band Boukman Eksperyans, and Massachusetts State House Representative Marie St. Fleur, who are oftentimes seen at the forefront of Haitian things, be they demonstrations against INS policies toward Haitians or events of a more festive nature. Their sense of pride for Haiti is well captured in the remarks of Haitian-born Olden Polynice—NBA star, former center of the Utah Jazz and currently with the Los Angeles Clippers—presented at the sixth annual Haitian music award in 2002:

> You can beat us. You can ship us back to Haiti. You can even say we started AIDS, but we will keep fighting. It is in our nature to be a proud people.

Renowned Haitian American writer Edwidge Danticat in Miami. Courtesy of the *Haitian Times.*

Just like their elders of the first generation, they take great pride in their racial and ethnic origin and argue that Haitians are capable of great achievements just as any other White immigrant group. They unremittingly go after the opportunities that the United States offers and are determined to succeed and overcome the hardest obstacles. Many second-generation Haitian immigrants believe that they have the power to shape their own destinies and argue that they should not wait for things to be given to them.

However, some also tend to share several of the first generation's negative opinions of certain members of the Black American community, who exhibit reprehensible behavior. Generally speaking, these include Haitians of more modest backgrounds who come in constant contact with lower-class African Americans in their neighborhoods. In their view, this undesirable behavior is characterized by a lack of respect for adults and authority, a lack of motivation to succeed and a certain disinterest in education, a desire to always make excuses, nonstop blaming of the White man for their misfortune, stealing, substance abuse, and teenage pregnancy. When it is pointed out that those characteristics are also found among Haitian youth, many second generation immigrants are quick to reply that Haitians, generally speaking, are good by nature but unfortunately have allowed themselves to be contaminated by others. The following statements are illustrative of their opinions of some African American youth: *Ou pa t ap janm wè timoun Ayisyen fè bagay konsa* (you would never see Haitian kids do that kind of stuff), *timoun Ameriken sa yo, se pa de vakabon yo vakabon, non* (those American kids, they are so "good-for-nothing"), *mwen menm, mwen pa boule ak yo* (myself, I don't deal with them).[14] In sum, the same tendency to disaffiliate oneself with members of the African American community, in particular, is present in the second generation, but it needs to be understood that it is class based. Common folks are more critical of Black Americans than privileged members, who forge alliances with African Americans in their quest for success. It also needs to be understood that prominent members of the second generation, although firmly rooted in the Haitian experience, can also be equally knowledgeable about American perspectives. This knowledge is used in dealing with U.S. institutions to advance themselves and the cause of their Haitian and Haitian American brothers who have not yet achieved the American dream. Moreover, there is some level of interethnic marriage between members of the Haitian immigrant second generation and those of the African American population (as well as those of other ethnic groups, for that matter). As the Haitian diasporic community continues to receive scholarly attention, the topic of interracial and interethnic marriage will undoubtedly be studied in some detail.

Weaker Form of Haitianness

Individuals located at this particular pole of the continuum are bicultural in the sense that neither culture is alien to them; but it is with regard to their involvement in and knowledge of Haitian matters that they differ from those who display a stronger form of Haitianness. In the discussion of ethnicity among second generation Haitian immigrants, various parameters should be considered, such as language preference and proficiency, ethnic designation, knowledge of Haitian and American cultures, opinions of various Haitian and American cultural aspects, and patterns of friendship and social interactions. Bicultural Haitians vary with regard to their acceptance of these cultural parameters and the degree to which they manifest their cultural allegiances to the two cultures.

Second-generation Haitian immigrants who are positioned at the weaker end of the Haitianness axis define themselves as *Haitian Americans*. Various factors can account for this choice of an ethnic identification. First, the fact that they were born in the United States or have been living here from a tender age (two to six) has given them a thorough knowledge of the American way of life that, in many instances, surpasses that of the Haitian way of life. Second, their lack of a foreign accent prevents them from sounding Haitian. Third, they have a greater level of proficiency in English than in Haitian Creole. Fourth, the fact that they have never been to Haiti, or stayed there for any significant amount of time (in several cases), precludes them from having firsthand information on the various facets of Haitian society and Haitian life in the homeland. Their understanding of what Haiti is about, unlike that of their parents, does not come from their having experienced for themselves the multiple realities of Haiti. Because of all these factors, they acknowledge a great deal of familiarity and ease with the American way and feel that the United States is their home. For them Haiti is linked to heritage, ancestry, and roots—the United States, to everyday reality.

Placed in this context, the label *Haitian American* could well mean an *American* who is very much aware of and accepts his or her Haitian ancestry. As such, members of this group do not hide the fact that they are of Haitian descent; on the contrary, they make it a point to tell their friends that their parents were born in Haiti and they do not manifest any shame toward their ancestors' land of origin. Moreover, although they are more proficient in English and claim it as their native language, they all have, at the very least, a passive knowledge of Haitian Creole that enables them to follow a conversation in that language and understand the gist of what is said around them, at home or in the Haitian community. Additionally, these Haitian Americans like several elements of Haitian culture, such as food, music, outgoingness, joviality, sense of pride, and a natural inclination toward optimism reflected in the Haitian saying *Bondye bon* (God is good). They further appreciate aspects of Haitian community life that reflect a genuine concern for the welfare of others and a sense of sharing. They also admire the sense of purpose of Haitian immigrants and their willingness to work hard in order to improve their lives and that of their family.

However, these individuals overall are less involved with Haitian diasporic matters, as well as those of the homeland. For example, in the course of a one-to-five-year timeframe, many would admit not having attended any Haitian community events (except immediate family gatherings), although they do not live far (less than 30 miles) from where these events take place.[15] When questioned about their absences, say at the *Konpa* festival, the various activities of Haitian Flag Day, or the numerous *bals* (dances/balls) organized by popular Haitian bands, Tabou Combo, T-Vice, and Boukman Ekspeyans, to recall a few, they would say that they did not feel like attending. Moreover, they do not keep abreast of the burning issues in the Haitian community, for example the situation of the boat people and INS policies pertaining to Haitian immigrants. Additionally, they do not know much about Haitian diasporic media or leading Haitian organizations. While it can be argued that some members of the first generation do not participate in Haitian affairs either, they, nevertheless, have a Haitian lifestyle at home that is absent from the daily existence of members of the second generation who display a weak form of Haitianness. These first-generation Haitian "homebodies" cook *à l'haïtienne,* purchase Haitian produce at the grocery store, speak Creole at home, listen to Haitian radio programs, are interested in Haitian neighborhood gossip, and socially interact only with Haitians. Contrary to their elders, the second generation (in the weaker category) is more detached from Haitian things. They are quite comfortable with American things, and they interact a great deal with members of other ethnic groups, including African Americans, toward whom they show more tolerance. Some may even disagree with how the elders react to American perspectives, in general, and resent their inability to understand that things are done differently in America. These things include, for example, allowing high schoolers to work, allowing girls to date at an earlier age (as opposed to 18 or 20), and more flexibility with curfew.

Denial of Haitianness

The denial of Haitianness or the undercover phenomenon is undoubtedly another manifestation of the various ethnic options available to second-generation Haitian immigrants, and it illustrates a trend that is totally different from the degrees of Haitianness discussed earlier. In its strongest form, the undercover phenomenon is a complete rupture from Haitianness and a strong inclination toward Black American monoculturalism. Undercover second-generation Haitian immigrants go to great length to conceal any trace of their Haitian identity, directly associated with Haiti. They endeavor to camouflage as much evidence of their Haitian origin as they can. For them, Haiti and Haitians are symbols of shame and embarrassment and constant reminders of a difficult past that must be discarded. Undercover Haitian youth believe that there is absolutely nothing to be gained from claiming any sort of Haitianness. On the contrary, they are convinced that it is an invitation to be ridiculed, to be labeled, to be marginalized, and to be excluded altogether from meaningful participation in American life. Covering up their Haitian ethnicity has become a strategy adopted by some Haitian youth to

deal with the cruel reality of ethnic prejudice that is still very pervasive in the
United States, particularly as far as recent immigrants from the Third World
are concerned. Moreover, the negative images associated with Haitians in the
U.S. media and the numerous instances of discrimination against Haitians on
the part of some Americans (and other groups) reinforce their desire to shed
their Haitian skins and to take on new identities that they hope will insulate
them from social ostracism and continuing attacks, particularly in school.
Their new identities highly correlate with their individual characteristics.
Those who were born and raised in the United States, because of their lack of
distinctive foreign accents and their thorough knowledge of American cultural practices, claim to be African Americans. For all intents and purposes,
they view themselves as Americans, and they have consciously chosen to rele-
gate Haiti and Haitian culture to a state of oblivion. As part of the American-
ization process, they modify both the spelling and pronunciation of their
names, going from Pierre to Peter, Michel to Michael, and Hervé to Herb.
Once this transformation is made, there is, indeed, very little left to distin-
guish them from the native group. Haitian youth who label themselves
African Americans are for the most part teenagers enrolled in the public
schools who are strongly influenced by peer pressure and a desire to belong.
They do not perceive an ethnic identity as important to their self-image. In
fact, as has been pointed out, some young Haitians reject parental control and
even seem to believe the negative stereotypes attached to Haitians. In consequence, they deny their Haitian identity, and "in many cases, model their
behavior and attitudes upon those of inner-city African Americans."[16] Those
who were born and reared in Haiti, for whom it is more difficult to camouflage traces of foreignness, claim that they have recently moved to the United
States after having lived for a long time in another Caribbean island, Canada,
or France. In some instances, they claim these countries as their birthplace as
well. These particular youngsters also fabricate an entirely new family history.
The more extreme fabrications make them sons and daughters of Caribbean
or African immigrants; and the more moderate stories portray them as offspring of first-generation Haitian immigrants who migrated a long time ago
and have not returned to the homeland since. This alleged, prolonged stay in
Canada or France is intended to erase any direct connection to Haiti and
association with the boat people, which, in their view, can only result in
heightened discrimination against them. Therefore, claiming to be a Haitian
Canadian or a Haitian French immigrant is perceived to be a more desirable
ethnic choice than simply being a Haitian immigrant. Moreover, they hold
the belief that these new identities can attenuate perceptions of poverty, igno-
rance, and backwardness generally associated with Haiti, but never with

Canada or France, which, on the contrary, generate rather positive feelings on the part of Americans.

Indeed, some second-generation Haitian immigrants find themselves in a most difficult position. At school, they are afraid of being too foreign, and they fear the negative consequences of their foreignness. Yet, at the same time at home, they are too "African American" and have to face the constant disapproval of their parents, who are not enamored of so-called African American behavior, as was discussed earlier. In many cases, youngsters seek to resolve their dilemma by estranging themselves completely from ethnicity and by devoting all their energies to erasing their supposed foreignness in order to fit in at school. It remains to be seen whether this strategy really works and enables these youngsters to advance in American society. Moreover, there is some evidence to suggest that once these teenagers graduate from high school and are no longer subjected to peer pressure, some rediscover their Haitian roots and feel differently about their Haitian ancestry.[17] Further, it is not at all obvious that undercover Haitian Americans have been able to discard the load of the past once and for all. Indeed, "to appreciate the tragic predicament in which some of [them] found themselves, it suffices to point out that the more intensely they despised their ethnic heritage the more conscious they were of their ethnic identity. The more ashamed they were of this past, and even of their parents, the more they were aware of their ethnic background."[18]

Ethnic identity within the Haitian diaspora is a concept constructed on foreign land as a means of adjusting to unfamiliar realities. Given the very circumstances that shape this particular construct, Haitian ethnicity is by definition transnational and mixed, composed of both native and foreign elements. By its very nature, it is also an unfinished product, which continues to evolve and is constantly being molded by new elements, resulting from the contact with other cultures and other people. Perhaps to describe the character of Haitian diasporic identity, one might have to accept its hybridity—more than one language, more than one ideal, more than one thought, more than one way of being human—all of this encapsulated in an African soul that has been creolized by the forces of history: colonialism, slavery, revolution, nationhood, and immigration.

OVERALL ASSESSMENT OF ADJUSTMENT AND ADAPTATION

In forty years or so, Haitian immigrants have come a long way in establishing themselves as visible ethnic communities in the United States. From New

York and Boston to Miami and Chicago, Haitians are changing the American landscape and incorporating themselves in the contemporary fabric of this country. From very humble beginnings, the Haitian diaspora has made significant progress, as evidenced by the well-known success of some of its members, many of whom were mentioned by name in chapter 5. Moreover, the visibility of this community can be seen in the fact that it is gradually receiving social and cultural recognition from mainstream U.S. institutions, and state and local governments that are recognizing its impact on American life. Another example of this sort of recognition can be seen in initiatives undertaken by the Smithsonian Institute in Washington, D.C., to commemorate the bicentennial of Haitian independence in 2004. At the time of this writing, preparations were under way for the 2004 Smithsonian Folklife Festival, seeking to bring the arts, music, foods, storytelling, history, and rich craft traditions of Haiti to an expected one million visitors. The festival, "Haiti: Freedom and Creativity . . . From the Mountains to the Sea," is perhaps the largest event organized in the United States in a year-long series of activities in commemoration of the 200th anniversary of the Haitian revolution and independence. According to Geri Benoit, head of the Haitian National Commission for the Bicentennial Celebration, the program "presents a prime opportunity to showcase the cultural creativity of the Haitian people as an expression of their passion for freedom and liberty."[19] It is intended to educate the general public about Haitian history, culture, and achievements. Senators Christopher Dodd of Connecticut and Mike DeWine of Ohio chaired the program committee on Haiti, which also included Senator Hillary Clinton of New York.[20] In addition, the fact that Haitian immigrants are the object of contemporary academic discourse and that Haitian perspectives are finding their way into school and college curricula is a further testament to the community's presence. Whatever success Haitian immigrants have thus far achieved is due to their strong sense of self-worth and purpose as immigrants, and their resiliency. Moreover, the strong importance they attach to education cannot be minimized, which is also one of the strongest values they transmit to the younger generation. Second-generation immigrant Gary Charles Eugene, the first Haitian commander in the City of Miami Police Department (attached to Little Haiti), recently explained in an interview with the *Haitian Times* why education is a priority:

> When you are Haitian, you are black, and you're an immigrant—that's three strikes against you. . . . You need to be prepared so that when you [reach a position], people don't say they "gave" it to you. They will say you earned it.[21]

His statement illustrates how all Haitian parents feel about education and explains why they are so determined to make all kinds of sacrifices to ensure that their offspring get a solid education. Only through education do they believe that Haitian immigrants can earn the prosperity and dignity they hope to gain in the United States. The number of Haitian Americans enrolling in and graduating every year from colleges and universities around the country is a clear indication that the American dream is accessible to them as well.

NOTES

1. For more on the definition of *generation,* see Alba (1990: 5) and Edmonston and Passel (1994: 321–22).

2. The numbers presented here are to be interpreted only in general terms. Certainly, one can find members of the second generation who are over 40. One can also note that these numbers are slightly different from those presented in Zéphir (2001). The earlier work looked at INS records until 1996, whereas the current work includes records through 2002. Immigration patterns for more recent years account for the slight difference.

3. Charles (1990: 13).

4. Basch, Glick Schiller, and Szanton Blanc (1994: 185).

5. Some of the points presented in this section were discussed in Zéphir (1996: chap. 3).

6. Laguerre (1984: 157).

7. All first-generation informants quoted in this section were interviewed in the context of fieldwork conducted in New York City in 1994 and 1998. See also Zéphir (1996: chap. 3).

8. For a more detailed discussion, see Zéphir (1997).

9. Charles (1990: 257).

10. Ibid., p. 296.

11. A last perusal of the *Cruising into History* Web site in May 2004 confirmed that the cruise would still be on.

12. For a more complete discussion of the second-generation Haitian immigrants, see Zéphir (2001).

13. Waters (1996: 178).

14. These statements were collected in the context of fieldwork conducted in New York City in 1998. See also Zéphir (2001).

15. Opinions expressed by these second-generation Haitian immigrants were collected in the context of fieldwork conducted with the Haitian diaspora of Miami, Boston, and Chicago in the summer of 2002.

16. Nachman (1997: 118–19).

17. Zéphir (2001, chap. 4).

18. Nahirny and Fishman (1996: 267–73).

19. As quoted on the following Haitian Web site: http://www.intermediahaiti.com.

20. A last perusal of the Smithsonian Institute's Web site in May 2004 confirmed that the festival would take place at the National Mall from June 23 to June 27 and from June 30 to July 4, 2004.

21. As quoted in the *Haitian Times* (July 30–August 5, 2003, front page).

7

Haitian Impact on American Society

The portrait of Haitian immigrants that was presented throughout the book demonstrates that this particular ethnic group has forever inscribed its images into the American tapestry. In just four decades, the Haitian diaspora has reached a certain degree of empowerment and has become a significant component of the fabric of contemporary American society. The journey of the Haitian people, from their enslavement on the plantations of Saint-Domingue, to their rise as the first Black republic of the world, to their designation as the poorest country of the Western Hemisphere, to their problematic status as boat people defying U.S. immigration laws, to their reasonably successful insertion into mainstream America, attests to their resiliency and their ability to survive. Haitians have proven that "they have the ability to live through the best of times and the worst of times."[1] The fortitude of their spirit is well captured in a poem written by Haitian American Marguerite Laurent in November 2002, after another boat load of two hundred people tried to reach the Miami shores as their boat ran aground. On that boat was a little girl in a yellow Sunday dress, whom television images around the country poignantly captured:

I saw you, little girl on CNN
A yellow butterfly, hanging by one arm
over the side of an overloaded with hopes
Haitian boat...
You're not facing the Atlantic will alone.

Nou la [We are here].
When you're unconquerable within,
all the forces of hell cannot
prevail against you from without.
We Haitians are there with you
even if it's not allowed.
Our spirit can never be chained,
contained or deterred.
Use your legacy, little Haitian girl...
The Lwas [spirits] cannot be chained,
contained or deterred...
No one holds your soul...[2]

The story of the Haitian diaspora in the United States documents that their spirits cannot be chained; they have within them the power to endure and to overcome adversity. Collectively, Haitians have proven that, when given an opportunity, they can achieve the highest level of success and become productive members of society, leaving their marks in their respective fields and places of employment and commanding the respect of their colleagues and coworkers. In fact, the notoriety that some Haitian Americans have achieved has made them American and even world icons.

HAITIAN AMERICAN CELEBRITIES

The entertainment and sport industries are perhaps the two domains where the majority of readers may have had an opportunity to appreciate the talents of such icons. It is perhaps appropriate to devote some attention to these Haitian celebrities, who have become household names in the United States.

Hip-hop artist Wyclef Jean is arguably the most recognizable second-generation Haitian immigrant. Many American youth (Black and White) know more about his music than Haitian immigrants themselves. Multiple Web sites are devoted to his albums; he can be seen on MTV and major television networks, including CNN. In fact, as late as December 2003, he gave an interview on National Public Radio. Clef (as he is known to his fans) was born on October 17, 1969, in the impoverished town of Croix-des-Bouquets outside of Port-au-Prince, in humble circumstances. He came to the United States at the age of nine and lived in the Brooklyn Marlborough Project. Subsequently he moved to New Jersey, where he attended high school. Wyclef made his debut with the Fugees—a name that is a short for the word *refugees,* chosen at a time when Haitian refugees were stacked up in Guantanamo Bay, Cuba. The group's first album, *Blunted on Reality,* came out in 1993. Wyclef, along with the other two Fugees members, Lauryn Hill and his cousin Prakazrel "Pras" Michel, rocketed to fame with their second album, *The Score,* one of the largest-selling and most influential hip-hop records in chart history, which earned a 1996 Grammy Award for Best Rap Album. In 1997, "the hip-hop Amadeus" released his first solo album, *The Carnival,* instantly becoming an American and perhaps a world icon. For this album, he collaborated with the Neville Brothers, recently deceased salsa icon Celia Cruz, and the New York Philharmonic. His other albums include *The Ecleftic* (2000), *The Masquerade* (2002), and *The Preacher's Son* (2003). Because of his fame, Wyclef transcends all races, nationalities, ethnicities, and social classes. Every teenager in the "hood" knows his music, raps his rap, and joins his Carnival. Yet he is just as well-known to the aristocrats and members of camelots. Indeed, no one needs to be reminded that Wyclef Jean performed a solo at the funeral of John Fitzgerald Kennedy, Jr., in July of 1999. In the words of Steve Desrosiers, a reporter for the *Haitian Boston Reporter* who interviewed Wyclef in April 2003, "as much as we want to try we really can't pin him nor just claim him for ourselves [Haitians]. He dines with presidents. He shoots movies in Jamaica. He leads fundraisers in Haiti. He writes lighthearted odes to strippers in the deep south. The latest? He's about to launch a World Music record label called *Sak Pase* Records (What's Happening Records)" (*Boston Haitian Reporter,* April 2003, p. 12). In short, American hip-hop music would not be what it is today without Wyclef Jean. Wyclef has proven to the world that genius transcends barriers, prejudices, and human bigotry. His impact on American society is immeasurable; he is one of the most important treasures of contemporary American and world music.

Another well-known second-generation Haitian American is actress Garcelle Beauvais. Like Wyclef Jean, numerous Web pages are devoted to her. Garcelle was born in Haiti on November 26, 1966, and moved to the United States as a young child. She is a household name to many television viewers around the country. Indeed, Garcelle is the leading star in two very popular television programs that have propelled her into the limelight: *The Jamie Foxx Show,* where she plays the role of Fransesca "Fancy" Monroe, and *NYPD Blue,* where she is Assistant District Attorney Valerie Heywood. She has also made appearances on a number of other popular TV shows, including *The Fresh Prince of Bel Air, The Cosby Show, Family Matters, Miami Vice,* and *Dream On.* Additionally, she has held roles in successful movies; in one of them, *Coming to America,* she costarred with Eddie Murphy. Moreover, Garcelle leads publicity campaigns for such cosmetics companies as Avon, Mary Kay, and Clairol. Her photographs are displayed in upscale department stores' catalogs such as Neiman Marcus and Nordstrom; she is featured in *Essence* and *Ebony* magazines. For all intents and purposes, Garcelle is known to her fans not as a *Haitian* actress but as a very talented *American* actress—one of their own—whom they enjoy seeing on television and in fashion shows and magazines. She too transcends race, ethnicity, and nationality. She has managed to carve for herself a successful place in the television industry, adding her talents to those of the best artists in the business.

In the sports arena, particularly in basketball, the best-known Haitian American athletes are undoubtedly Olden Polynice, former center of the Utah Jazz and currently with the Los Angeles Clippers, and Mario Elie, former star of the San Antonio Spurs, who contributed to the team's three NBA championships and who currently serves as its assistant coach. The successful career of these talented basketball players is well-known to the fans, and a record of their accomplishments can be found on numerous Web sites. Polynice and Elie are counted among the NBA's best and their prowess on the court is inscribed in the NBA's annals. As such, these Haitian American athletes are part of American sports' legacy.

Finally, one must add Marjorie Vincent to the list of Haitian celebrities, who was crowned Miss America 1991. Marjorie, the daughter of Haitian immigrants, was born in Illinois. A gifted classical pianist, she competed for the Miss America title on the platform of domestic violence. When she finished her illustrious reign, she went on to complete her college degree at Duke University. Subsequently, she began her professional career as a news anchor. Marjorie Vincent will always be remembered as an American daughter of exceptional beauty and grace, who represented her country with dignity and compassion. She is truly a role model to scores of young women who share the same dreams of being among the stars.

THE COMMON FOLKS

Haitian Americans comprise all sectors of American society; they belong to all walks of life. From the common folks to the celebrities just mentioned, they are all driven by a common desire to make a better life for themselves and their families. By migrating to the United States, they joined millions of immigrants who came before them in search of their basic inalienable rights: life, liberty, and the pursuit of happiness. In their determination to become productive members of American society and to live with dignity, they follow different career paths and choose different occupations. Indeed, Haitian American immigrants are our congressmen and congresswomen; they are the doctors and nurses who provide health care to us; they are the engineers who build our monuments, buildings, and highways; they are the teachers and professors who educate our youth; they are the police officers who make our streets and neighborhoods safer; they are the firemen and -women who brave danger to save our lives; they are the soldiers in the army who risk their lives to make our world a better place; they are the lawyers who defend our legal rights; they are the journalists who bring the news to our homes; they are our artists and entertainers; they are our neighborhoods' convenience store, restaurant, and barbershop owners; they are the cabbies who take us to our hotels; they are the maids who clean our hotel rooms; they are our colleagues, coworkers, and classmates. On the one hand, several Haitian Americans have names that are familiar to many readers. But on the other, they are countless others whose stories will never make national news; they are the unsung heroes of the Haitian American diasporic experience. It is fitting to mention some of them in this work. These heroes and heroines include, for example, Manhattan police officer Monode Bonheur, who was at the World Trade Center after the September 11 attack, sifting through the rubble in search of survivors; Marie Carme Jules, owner of Café Créole in Uniondale, Long Island; barber Saurel Bazelais, also of Uniondale; Mireille Pierre, a grocery store clerk in Elizabeth, New Jersey; Feret Fenelus, owner of a dry-cleaning shop, also in Elizabeth; Vera Lafosse, a 2003 graduate from the University of Miami; Marcel Jean-François, a taxi driver at Miami International Airport; Michelange Arty, owner of La Patisserie Bakery on Brooklyn's Nostrand Avenue; Eustache Mathurin, head of the choir at St. Matthew's Church in Dorchester, Boston; Kesnel Edouard, a volunteer ESL (English as a Second Language) teacher in Boston; Ron Apollon, girls director of coaching at Metro North Youth Soccer Club in Marietta, Georgia; and the frightened little "boat girl" in a yellow Sunday dress, who disembarked on the Miami shores in October 2002.

Haitian Americans we recognize for their contributions also include those whose violent deaths—parts of very tragic U.S. events—we mourn. On September 11, 2001, several were killed in the World Trade Center, one of them, André Bonheur, a Citibank financial analyst believed to be attending a meeting at Cantor Fitzgerald.[3] Among the many firefighters from the New York

City Fire Department were two Haitians, Gérard Baptiste and André Joseph, who lost their lives attempting to save those of others.[4] On October 3, 2002, 72-year-old Pascal Charlot was gunned down in the unprecedented shooting spree perpetrated by Lee Boyd Malvo that shook the nation's capital, becoming the sniper's sixth victim. His funeral service, conducted mostly in Haitian Creole at the Shrine of the Sacred Heart Roman Catholic Church in Washington, D.C., was attended by more than four hundred people, including Representative Connie Morella of Maryland, District of Columbia's delegate Eleanor Holmes Norton, and Mayor Anthony Williams.[5] On March 10, 2003, 36-year-old Haitian American detective James Némorin (along with his American partner Rodney Andrews) was gunned down and killed during an undercover operation in Staten Island. His death sent a chill throughout the police force in New York City. His funeral, held at the Lady of Refuge Church in Brooklyn, was attended by thousands of police officers who lined the streets of Brooklyn to bid farewell to their slain comrade. High-ranking city and state officials, including Mayor Michael Bloomberg and Police Commissioner Raymond Kelly, turned out to pay their final respects. In the words of another fellow officer, Némorin was "somebody who put his life on the line, so you could go home at night without worrying that someone is going to shoot you."[6] On June 28, 2003, tragedy struck again. Thirty-seven-year-old army sergeant Gladimir Philippe was found dead near Baghdad, after a three-day disappearance. Philippe was a 16-year veteran who joined the army in 1988 and served in the Persian Gulf War, in Bosnia, and in Haiti.[7]

In sum, no matter what sector of American society one chooses to look at, Haitians are there, making their contributions to American life. Although it is very difficult to have an accurate count of the number of Haitians who are incorporated in the various components of the labor force of this country—agriculture and forestry, mining and construction, manufacturing, communications, trade, financial services, professional services, and public administration—due mostly to the fact that they are subsumed under the category "Black" or "African American" in companies' records, it is nevertheless fair to claim that they have managed to penetrate all fields.

HAITIANS IN AMERICA: A CRITICAL MASS

At present, Haitian immigrants stand at nearly one million strong. They are here to stay; their children and grandchildren claim this land as theirs. Within one generation, Haitians have transformed major U.S. cities, among them unquestionably New York, Miami, and Boston, and to a great extent many others, including Newark (New Jersey), Philadelphia, Washington, D.C., Fort Lauderdale, West Palm Beach, Chicago, and Atlanta. In their areas of resettlement, they establish vibrant communities where they proudly display their allegiances to their ethnic culture. This allegiance is seen in their arts, their music, their food, their religious traditions, and their literature. The tangible beginning of their relocation process can be traced to 1957 when François "Papa Doc" Duvalier became president of Haiti. Shortly after, Haitians began their exodus to the United States and other countries around the world. The constant political chaos that has prevailed in Haiti all throughout its history has prevented the small nation from advancing economically. Those conditions have led, and continue to lead, to steady waves of both legal and illegal immigration.

Haitians' arrival provoked a large degree of "ethnocentric backlash," manifested in the tightening of immigration laws, the passing of discriminatory policies and regulations, and outright brutality.[8] Anti-Haitian sentiments flared all over the United States, particularly in the 1980s all throughout the 1990s, when the number of Haitians trying to reach the shores of the United States skyrocketed. Haitians were forbidden to donate blood and they were branded AIDS carriers. A culture of fear started, manifestations of which persist to the present day. Through it all, Haitians did not allow their spirits to be chained, contained, or deterred. They made the best of adversity, resolving to reclaim their Haitian image in American culture. To a great extent, their determination, and perhaps their legacy, have allowed them to overcome; their hard work is beginning to pay off. Several sectors of American society are gradually accepting the fact that Haitians are the new faces of America; they are no longer birds of passage. For example, in cities like New York, politicians are courting the Haitian community's votership. They are reaching out to community leaders and are beginning to listen to their concerns, in the hope of developing long-lasting ties and alliances with members of this particular ethnic community. Indeed, this makes good political sense. Likewise, city and state agencies are willing to offer friendlier services to Haitian immigrants by reaching them in their language, Haitian Creole, and by employing Haitian workers and professionals. Major corporations, among them American Airlines, Western Union, and AT&T, are realizing that Haitians are a significant consumer force to be reckoned with. In this connection, one can mention that on December 11, 2003, Western Union organized its First L'Union fait la force Awards Ceremony (Strength in Unity Awards) to acknowledge the achievements of notable Haitian Americans (some of whom are profiled in the Appendix). Haitian Americans have been appointed by governors, mayors, and other prominent government-elected officials to hold important positions in their offices. Moreover, Haitian Americans themselves have made some significant strides in politics and are beginning to find a sense of political identity in the United States, as evidenced by their winning seats in state congress (two in Florida and one in Massachusetts) and campaigning successfully in mayoral and judicial elections.[9] In the words of Florida State Representative Philipp Brutus, "clearly the Haitian community is evolving. Ten years ago, we could not have even thought about achieving this."[10] More evidence of the successful presence of Haitians in American society can be seen in the fact that major corporations (banks, accounting firms, insurance companies, and industries) are hiring Haitian American (or Haitian) professionals; law firms, Haitian American lawyers; school districts, Haitian American teachers; hospitals, Haitian American nurses and doctors; universities, Haitian American professors; and news agencies, Haitian American journalists, reporters, and news anchors.

Social scientists have long argued that for an immigrant to become American, he or she must be respected and accepted by the rest of the United States, by the established residents. They further stress that the process of

Senator Hillary Clinton courting the Haitian American votership during her 2000 campaign. She is pictured with the late Dr. Henry Victor Beaulieu and his wife, Islande Beaulieu. Courtesy of the *Haitian Times*.

acceptance and integration does not solely depend on what the immigrant group says or does. Rather it "unfolds from the interaction between immigrants and established Americans, those who were born and raised in the United States, who view themselves as the real or mainstream Americans."[11] The history of the relationships between Haitian immigrants and established or mainstream U.S. residents has been fraught with conflicts and is replete with instances of discrimination and hate. The Haitian community has had to engage in a great deal of social activism and establish quite a number of organizations and associations to advance its rights. Fiercely, Haitian immigrants took their cause to federal, city, and state officials and demanded justice and equality. They challenged the so-called established Americans to live up to the democratic ideals upon which this country was founded. From the late 1950s to 2004, the Haitian community has made some progress in the process of becoming "American" and being accepted by mainstream American society. There are signs that can lead to a certain degree of cautious optimism. Many Haitian Americans are successful and are known for their accomplishments in their respective fields (see Appendix for a profile of selected notable Haitian Americans). Further, Haitian visual and sacred arts are displayed at New York's Museum of Natural History and other museums around the country; Haitian heritage and folk traditions are accorded a place of prominence at the Smithsonian Folklife Festival; Haitians are represented in state and city governments; Haitian rhythms and dances are performed at Carnegie Hall; Haitian music resounds in huge American open spaces; American Haitian literature is taught at U.S. universities; and leading U.S. publishing houses are publishing works on Haitians and by Haitian authors. Perhaps the biggest impact of Haitian Americans in the United States is that they are contributing to creating what an Asian American scholar calls "a community of a larger memory."[12] As the Haitian community matures and as the second and third generations come of age, perhaps they will be seen as less alien and more American. After all, America is a permanently unfinished society, where the new and old always blend to produce a much larger and better nation, one out of many, "the varied carols of America."[13]

NOTES

1. Like the Dominican Americans described by Torres-Saillant and Hernández (1998: 158).

2. The poem, "An Open Letter to the Little Girl in the Yellow Sunday Dress," was published in its entirety in the *Boston Haitian Reporter* (January 2003, pp. 16–17).

3. See the *Haitian Times* front-page story, "Haitian Americans Missing after Attacks" (September 19–25, 2001, issue).

4. This information was provided by the Haitian Consulate in New York.

5. For more on this story, see the *Boston Haitian Reporter* (November 2002 issue).

6. As reported in the *Haitian Times* (March 19–25, 2003, issue, front page).

7. For more on this story, see the *Haitian Times* (July 2–8, 2003, issue, front page).

8. The term *ethnocentric backlash* is taken from Stepick et al. (2003: 11).

9. For more on Haitian political identity in South Florida, see Valbrun's article in the *Haitian Times* (January 2–8, 2002, issue, front page).

10. As quoted in the *Haitian Times* (January 2–8, 2002, issue, p. 4).

11. Stepick et al. (2003: 25–26).

12. Takaki (1998: 345).

13. The expression "varied carols" is from Walt Whitman's *Leaves of Grass* as quoted in Takaki (1998: prologue).

Appendix: Noted Haitian Americans

Marleine Bastien (1959–   ), a social worker and founder and executive director of Fanm Ayisyen nan Miami, Inc. (Haitian Women of Miami, also known as FANM), was born in Haiti. She immigrated to the United States in 1981. She first attended Miami-Dade County Community College and, subsequently, Florida International University, where she earned a bachelor and a master of science degree in social work in 1986 and 1987, respectively.

From 1982 to 1987, Bastien worked full-time as an interpreter and paralegal at the Haitian Refugee Center. She accompanied lawyers from the center to the Krome Detention Center, where thousands of Haitian refugees were held awaiting their immigration hearings. In 1987, Bastien began her career as a clinical social worker at Jackson Memorial Hospital in Miami. In 1991, she founded FANM, which was at the time a purely volunteer organization advocating Haitian women's rights. Over the years, her organization grew significantly and started attracting funding from important foundations for the meaningful work it was doing to give Haitian women a social, political, and economic voice. Under Bastien's leadership, FANM received a number of significant awards, such as the 1997 Best Non-Profit Organization of the Year from the Miami-Dade Chamber of Commerce. In addition, March 8, 1999, was declared Haitian Women of Miami Day by Miami's mayor, Alex Penelas. Subsequently in 2000, Bastien left Jackson Memorial Hospital to become the full-time executive director of the organization. She also serves on the board of a number of other important organizations, such as the Florida Immigrant Advocacy Center, the Health Foundation of South Florida, and the Women's Interface Network.

Bastien is considered by many the most vocal Haitian woman in the Miami area. She is, indeed, the spokesperson of the Haitian community and is always seen at the forefront of demonstrations for the rights of Haitian refugees. She is not afraid to take the Haitian cause to the nation's capital, where she is a powerful voice. Indeed, she spoke in Washington in October 2000 at the historic World March of Women. She is often quoted in local, national, and international media outlets, such as CNN, BBC, and the Oprah Winfrey show. For her social work and activism, Bastien has received many awards. Among the most recent ones are the Service Medallion Award from Florida International University, the W. E. B. Du Bois Award from the NAACP, the Social Worker of the Year Award from Miami-Dade County, the 2001 Woman of the Year Award by *Ms* Magazine, and the National Leadership for a Changing World Award from the Ford Foundation.

Philipp Brutus (1957–   ), a Florida state house representative, was born in Haiti. He came to the United States in 1972 and attended Erasmus Hall High School in Brooklyn, New York, where he graduated in 1976. Subsequently, he moved to Boston and enrolled at the University of Massachusetts, where he obtained a bachelor of science degree in criminal justice forensics and political science in 1982. He then went to Suffolk University Law School and earned his law degree in 1985.

Brutus moved to Florida and began his law career as the first Haitian American attorney appointed assistant federal public defender in Miami. He has been in private practice since 1988, specializing in personal injury, medical malpractice, and immigration and criminal defense. Brutus's desire to join the political arena started in 1994, when he ran unsuccessfully for a judgeship seat in the state of Florida. That same year, he was appointed by President Clinton to be part of a steering committee for the Summit of the Americas. In 2000, Brutus became the first Haitian American to be elected to the Florida legislature; he has been subsequently reelected.

Brutus is well-known in the Haitian community for his advocacy efforts on behalf of the Haitian refugees. His 21-day hunger strike in protest of the U.S. decision to allow Cuban refugees into this country while Haitians were sent back home earned him the visibility and respect of the community. For this public stance against unfair treatment, Brutus received an NAACP Freedom Award in 1992. He is a member of the Federal Trial Lawyers Association, the Academy of Florida Trial Lawyers, the National Academy of Criminal Defense Lawyers, and the Florida Bar Association. He is licensed to practice before the U.S. Court of International Trade. He also served as Associate General Council for the NAACP, where he handled pro bono cases. In the Florida

State House of Representatives, Brutus serves as the vice-chair of the Claims subcommittee; he is a member of the Judiciary, Commerce, and Natural Resources committees and of the subcommittees on Banking and Securities and on Public Lands and Water Resources. Brutus has been involved in an amendment that allows nonpermanent residents without valid visas to have a two-year driver's license while their cases are under review by immigration courts. In addition, he is credited for having successfully shepherded efforts to rename Miami's Little Haiti 54th Street, Boulevard Toussaint Louverture. The name change was approved and became effective in September 2003. Brutus is a sought-after speaker invited by many Haitian American organizations to talk about Haitian rights. He has been a member of a delegation of Haitian American, Caribbean, and American jurists, who visited Haiti to assess the state of its legal system.

Alix Cantave (1959–   ), an economic development planner and the founding president of the Haitian Studies Association (HSA), was born in Haiti. He came to the United States in 1974, and attended John Jay High School, in Brooklyn, New York, where he graduated in 1978. He obtained a bachelor of arts degree in environmental design from the State University of New York at Buffalo in 1983 and a master of science degree in city and regional planning from the Pratt Institute in Brooklyn in 1987. At the time of this writing, Cantave was completing his doctorate in public policy at the University of Massachusetts–Boston.

Cantave is best known in Haitian circles throughout the United States (and Haiti) for his leadership role in the Haitian Studies Association, which he was instrumental in establishing in 1988, when he relocated to Boston to serve as project manager for Economic Development for the City of Sommerville, Massachusetts, a position he held until 1994. Cantave's dream of bringing Haitian matters into mainstream academic and political discourse materialized in the halls of Tufts University, where leading public policy scholar Robert Rotberg was at the time vice president for the College of Arts, Humanities and Science. Cantave contacted Rotberg, who agreed to support the establishment of a Haitian Studies Association at Tufts University.

Cantave served as the founding president of HSA from 1989 to 1993 and has remained to date one of the most valuable members of the association, responsible for its solid reputation as a scholarly organization that brings together professionals to discuss issues affecting Haiti and Haitians from a multidisciplinary perspective. Cantave is credited for having skillfully planned and organized the first 10 HSA annual conferences (1989–1999); he also served as the first editor of the *Journal of Haitian Studies,* arguably the premier journal in the field. In 1994, HSA moved to the University of Massachu-setts–Boston and received a major grant from the Ford Foundation to work on issues of education, governance, environment, and development. Cantave became the HSA/Haitian Studies project director until 1999, when he left to take the position of economic development program officer for the Local Initiatives Support Corporation. Given his expertise in economic development and nongovernmental organizations, Cantave is a sought-after speaker invited to lecture on these topics throughout the United States and Haiti. For his numerous contributions, Cantave has received an award from the American Planning Association and the Outstanding Service Award from the Haitian Studies Association.

Josaphat (Joe) Celestin (1956–), the mayor of the City of North Miami, was born in Haiti. He received his early training in civil engineering from the State University of Haiti before immigrating to the United States in 1978. In Florida, Celestin pursued a career in land engineering and construction management and earned several state certifications in business, finance, project management, general construction, and commercial and residential real estate development. In 1998, he received a master of science degree in architecture from the Florida University system.

Prior to becoming in 2001 the first Haitian American to ever become mayor of a U.S. city and the first Black to be elected mayor of the City of North Miami, Celestin was known throughout the Southern Florida community for his entrepreneurship. He is the chairman of Joe Celestin Civil Engineering and General Builder Company, which is involved in a variety of redevelopment projects sponsored by the government office of Housing and Urban Development (HUD). Celestin has always been involved in city politics and has had appointments on a number of important boards, including the North Miami Board of Adjustment, the North Miami Planning Commission, the City of Miami Finance and Budget Review Committee, the North Miami Hospital Board, and the Metropolitan Planning Organization, among many others. In addition, he served as a member of the Presidential Meritorious Rank Review Board in 1997 under the Clinton administration. Celestin is also the founder and chairman of the Haitian American Political Action Committee (HAPAC), which is composed of politically active and prominent Haitian Americans who examine potential local and state offices for which Haitians should run. He is also the founder of the Haitian-American Republican Club, whose membership is around 3,000 Haitians.

As mayor, Celestin is at the forefront of equality and fair housing for all. He plays a prominent role in the Biscayne Landing Redevelopment Project, which is a public and private venture in cooperation with the City of North Miami to develop approximately 190 acres of land in the heart of North Miami. He has also been instrumental in the negotiations undertaken with Savannah Mayor Floyd Adams, Jr., to allocate parkland to the Haitian Historical Society for the construction of a monument to commemorate Haitians' involvement in the Battle of Savannah. Celestin's major awards include the Noble Award from the National Organization for the Law Enforcement of the United States, a Citation from the National Black Police Association, and the Florida Agricultural and Mechanical University (A&M) Excellence in Government and Law Award.

Edwidge Danticat (1969–   ), arguably the most prominent Haitian American writer, was born in Haiti. She came to the United States in 1981 and graduated from Clara Barton High School in Brooklyn, New York, in 1986. She earned a bachelor of arts degree in French translation and literature from Columbia University's Barnard College, graduating magna cum laude in 1990. Subsequently, she went to Brown University and earned a master of fine arts degree in creative writing in 1993.

Only in her mid-thirties, Danticat has already published an impressive body of works, comprising some forty essays and short stories and several acclaimed novels. Among these are *Breath, Eyes, Memory* (1994), chosen by Oprah Winfrey for her book club in 1998; *Krik Krak* (1995), a finalist for the National Book Award; *The Farming of Bones* (1998), which won the America Book Award; *After the Dance: A Walk through Carnival in Jacmel, Haiti* (2002); *Behind the Mountains* (2002), named Book for the Teen Age by the New York Public Library and the Americas' Children and Young Adult Literature Honor Book; and *Dew Breaker* (2004). She has edited several collections of short stories, among them *The Butterfly's Way: Voices from the Haitian Dyaspora in the United States* (2001) and *Beacon Best of 2000: Great Writing by Men and Women of All Colors.* She has also worked with movie director, producer, and writer Jonathan Demme; she was featured in his film *Beloved.* In addition, Danticat has held professorship positions in departments of English and creative writing programs at several universities, including New York University, Brown University, Texas A&M University, and the University of Miami. Moreover, Danticat is very involved in the Haitian community, regularly organizing cultural programs and speaking to Haitian children and teenagers in the public schools. She works closely with Haitian American organizations and associations and lends her visibility to advance the cause of the Haitian refugees.

Danticat has been profiled in several newspapers and magazines around the country, including the *Washington Post Book World,* the *New Times Book Review,* the *Boston Globe, Newsweek,* the *Seattle Times, USA Today,* the *Haitian Times,* the *Boston Haitian Reporter, Essence* magazine, and *Harper's Bazaar* magazine, which calls her "One of the 33 Women of the 21st Century." For her accomplishments, Danticat has received several prestigious awards: the Pushcart Prize for Short Fiction, the Lila Wallace Reader's Digest Writers Award, the 20th Century New Voice Award from the organization of Women Writers of Africa, and the Carbet Literature Prize of the Caribbean.

Sybil Elias, a municipal court judge in East Orange, New Jersey, was born and raised in New Jersey. After obtaining her high school diploma from Union Catholic High School in Scotch Plains, New Jersey, she went to Rutgers University where she obtained a bachelor of arts degree in political science in 1994 and earned a certification in American politics from the Eagleton Institute of Politics in New Brunswick. She subsequently went to George Washington University Law School and earned her law degree in 1997. That same year, she was admitted to the New Jersey Bar. While in law school, she attended Oxford University in England where she received a certificate in International Human Rights Law and Refugee/Immigration Law in 1996. She also attended the National College of District Attorneys in Columbia, South Carolina, and received certifications in Juvenile Justice and Trial Advocacy.

Immediately after receiving her law degree, Elias began her legal career as a law clerk, first for the Honorable Irvin B. Booker and subsequently for the Honorable Harold Fullilove and the Honorable Donald Goldman. In that capacity, she worked on a number of cases regarding child custody, parental rights, alimony, and domestic violence. Upon Judge Booker's retirement, Elias cofounded the Irvin B. Booker Scholarship Fund benefiting college-bound high school seniors from the greater-Newark area. From September 1998 to January 2002, Elias served as assistant prosecutor for Essex County, New Jersey, where she litigated criminal cases, supervised legal investigations, and negotiated plea bargains. In addition, she represented the Prosecutor's Office at countless community board meetings and speaker's bureaus. In February 2002, Elias established her private practice, specializing in nonprofit organizations. In 2003, she was nominated by the mayor of East Orange for a judgeship to the East Orange Municipal Court. She was confirmed by the city council and sworn in on June 17, 2003, as East Orange's first judge of Haitian descent. She is also the youngest Haitian American to hold such an important position in the U.S. judicial system. Elias belongs to a number of professional organizations, including the American Bar Association, the National Bar Association, and the Garden State Bar Association.

In addition to her work on the bench, Elias is well-known in the New Jersey area for her volunteer work with the Newark Program for Acceleration of Careers in Engineering (PACE). As coadministrator of the PACE Youth Development program, she has played an integral part in its development by expanding the local Newark chapter to mentor and tutor 8th to 12th graders interested in the fields of law, computer science, and journalism. She regularly conducts lectures and workshops for college-bound high school achievers interested in these disciplines. In addition, she serves as a legal coach for the New Jersey State Bar Foundation. In this role, she prepares 9th graders to compete for a statewide mock trial competition. Elias is truly one of the pillars of the New Jersey community. For her outstanding achievements, in 2003 she received an award from the National Black Prosecutor's Association and an Outstanding Citizen Award from the Haitian League.

Carole Bérotte Joseph (1949–   ), a well-known educator and dean of Academic Affairs at Dutchess Community College in Poughkeepsie, New York, was born in Haiti. She came to the United States in 1957 and graduated from All Saints High School in Brooklyn, New York, in 1967. She earned a bachelor of arts degree (cum laude) in Spanish and education from York College of the City University of New York in 1971 and a master of science (magna cum laude) in curriculum and teaching and in bilingual education from Fordham University in 1975. Subsequently, she went on to earn a Ph.D. in bilingual education and sociolinguistics from New York University in 1992.

Joseph is a seasoned educator whose rich and varied career spans over three decades. In the early 1970s, she began her career as an elementary Spanish bilingual teacher and a junior high school Spanish and French teacher. In 1975, she moved to higher education, as an adjunct lecturer in the Bilingual Education Program at the City College of the City University of New York. Within a year she became a full-time faculty member; there she was instrumental in the development of bilingual education programs for Haitian immigrant students enrolled in the New York City public schools and the training of qualified teachers to work in these programs. In 1981, with a substantive grant from the New York State Department of Education, she founded the Haitian Parent and Teacher Training project (HAPTT) at City College to train the first cadre of Haitian bilingual teachers in the country. When she became assistant dean of the Department of Education and director of Student Services, she managed to secure additional funds to establish the Haitian Bilingual Technical Assistance Center (HABETAC) at City College to offer technical assistance to school districts involved with Haitian immigrant education throughout New York State. In 1996, Joseph went to Hostos Community College (in the Bronx) to serve as associate dean of Academic Affairs. Two years later she quickly rose to the position of vice president for Academic Affairs, a position she held until 2000 when she left to become dean of Academic Affairs and chief academic officer at Dutchess Community College of the State University of New York. Joseph belongs to a number of important organizations, including the National Association for Bilingual Education, the National Association for Multicultural Education, and the Haitian Studies Association, of which she is the immediate past president. She is also involved in a great deal of community service with the American Red Cross, the United Way, the Haitian American Cultural and Social Organization (HASCO), and the Haitian American United for Progress Community Center (HAUP). She supports humanitarian work in Haiti as well.

Joseph is well-known to Haitian teachers throughout the country, and she is often invited to conduct workshops dealing with Haitian education. She has appeared on various radio and television broadcasts, including National Public Radio and the *Geraldo Rivera Show*, to discuss educational issues of relevance to minority communities in the United States. Among her most prestigious awards are the 1995 Educator of the Year Gladys Correa Award from the New York State Association for Bilingual Education, the Haitian American Connections Award from the U.S. ambassador to Haiti, and the Distinguished Educator Award from the Haitian American Alliance. In December 2003, she received a Strength in Unity Award from Western Union.

Margareth Jourdan (1961–), a village judge in Spring Valley in Rockland County, New York, was born in Haiti. She came to the United States in 1972 and settled in New York. She graduated from Erasmus Hall High School in Brooklyn, New York, in 1979. She went to Hunter College of the City University of New York, where she earned a bachelor's degree in psychology in 1985. She subsequently went to the City University School of Law at Queens College and received her law degree in 1989.

Prior to entering the political arena, Jourdan practiced as a public interest attorney in the private and nonprofit sectors, doing mostly civil rights, immigrant rights, and immigration work. She also clerked for a supervising administrative law judge at the New York State Department of Social Services. From December 1997 to June 2001, Jourdan served as trustee, a legislative position, for the Village of Spring Valley. She was the first Haitian American elected to that position. In addition, she served as an assistant to the chairman of the

Rockland County legislature. In May 2001, Jourdan was nominated by Mayor Allan A. Thompson to sit and complete an unexpired term in the Village of Spring Valley. She was sworn-in in June 2001 by New York Governor George Pataki. Six months later, she successfully ran for the right to retain her seat, becoming the first woman judge of African heritage to hold this position in Rockland County's two hundred years of history. Jourdan is also the first Haitian American to ever hold an elected seat in the state of New York.

In addition to serving as an elected official, Jourdan plays an active role in the Rockland County public schools. She volunteers her time as junior achievement consultant to teach the fundamentals of free enterprise in various elementary schools. She also lectures extensively on civic duties and constitutional and immigrant rights. She is a strong advocate for the Haitian immigrant population of Rockland County. She is a member of the New Jersey Bar Association and the Rockland County Black Bar Association. For her accomplishments and public service, Jourdan has received several awards and several proclamations from the Council of the City of New York, and keys to the City of Miami-Dade County.

Jocelyn (Johnny) McCalla (1955–   ), the executive director of the National Coalition for Haitian Rights (NCHR), was born in Haiti. He immigrated to the United States in 1968 and attended Jamaica High School in Queens, New York, where he graduated in 1972. Subsequently, he enrolled in an engineering program at City College of the City University of New York, but eventually abandoned the program after three years to "join the revolution," as he jokingly says. The "revolution" in question is the advancement of international human rights in general, and Haitian rights in particular.

McCalla is well-known throughout the Haitian diasporic community of the United States for his relentless fight for social justice. His name is synonymous with Haitian rights. From the Haitian neighborhoods of New York, New Jersey, Miami, Boston, Chicago, and Atlanta to the higher echelons of the Congress of the United States in Washington, D.C., McCalla's forceful voice resounds. The major part of his public life has been devoted to the plight of Haitian refugees and asylum-seekers. From 1986 to 1988, he served as associate director of the National Coalition for Haitian Refugees (NCHR, as the organization was called at the time) and then from 1988 to 2002 as the organization's executive director. After a year hiatus, when he went to Africa to work on HIV/AIDS-related projects under the auspices of the African Jesuit AIDS Network (AJAN), McCalla returned to his New York–based position as executive director of NHCR in November 2003. Under McCalla's leadership, the National Coalition for Haitian Refugees/Rights immersed itself in several campaigns and legal efforts to protect the rights of Haitian refugees under international and U.S. law and to promote human rights and democratic governance in Haiti. As part of such efforts, McCalla launched *Haiti Insight,* a monthly news bulletin that quickly became a key resource for the media, advocates, lawyers, asylum officers, and policy- and lawmakers concerned with developments in Haiti. Working with a broad group of key civil rights, labor, religious, and immigrant and human rights advocates, NCHR led major initiatives that, in 1986 and 1998, resulted in legislative remedies that collectively allowed some 90,000 Haitian refugees to gain legal immigrant status in the United States. In 1991, NCHR deepened its commitment to human rights in Haiti by opening a field office that, in addition to promoting human rights, trained Haitian human rights advocates and informed the work of the United Nations Human Rights Mission in Haiti. NCHR's office in Haiti is the country's leading human rights voice. In 1995, McCalla reengineered NCHR as the National Coalition for Haitian *Rights,* shifting the organization's focus from a refugee-protection agenda to a broader domestic (U.S.) rights agenda.

During his tenure as NCHR's executive director, McCalla has been featured in such network and cable news broadcasts as the *McNeil-Lehrer News Hour,* ABC News *Nightline,* WNBC's the *Today Show,* the *McCreary Report,* and CNN, among others. He has also been quoted in the *New York Times,* the *Washington Post,* the *Wall Street Journal, USA Today, New York Newsday,* the *Miami Herald,* and the *Chicago Tribune.* McCalla is a member of the Board of Human Rights Watch/Americas, the Haitian Studies Association, and the Global Information Network. He has edited, authored, or coauthored numerous reports on human rights conditions in Haiti. Among the most recent ones are *The Odyssey of Haitian Refugees* (1995), *Restavèk No More: Eliminating Child Slavery in Haiti* (2002), and *Challenges Before the Haitian Diaspora* (2003). He is a recipient of a Western Union 2003 Strength in Unity Award.

Rudolph Moise (1954–), a well-known medical doctor specializing in pain management and an entrepreneur in the Miami community, was born in Haiti. He came to the United States in 1971. In 1977, he received a bachelor of arts degree from the University of Illinois at Chicago. Subsequently, in 1981, he went on to earn a doctorate in osteopathy (DO) from the Chicago College of Osteopathic Medicine. In 1994, he earned a master's degree in business administration from the University of Miami, and in 1997, he earned a law degree from the same institution. Additionally, he trained at the U.S. Air Force School of Aerospace Medicine; he is a flight surgeon who holds the rank of lieutenant colonel in the U.S. Air Force Reserve.

Moise is one of the most recognizable members of the Haitian diaspora in the United States, as he juggles many careers and professional endeavors. Indeed, he is the owner of a medical center, the Comprehensive Health Center, the president of the Miami-Dade Ambulance Service, and the president and CEO of a Miami-based Haitian broadcasting network, Radio Carnivale. He has also added acting to his credentials; he was featured as a Haitian attorney in the first Haitian independent movie, *Wind of Desire,* shown recently in U.S. movie theaters. Moise is well-known in the Greater Miami area for his civic participation and has been a member of important boards, including the University of Miami Board of Trustees, the United Way Board of Directors, the Immigration Emergency Fund Advisory Committee, and the Greater Miami Chamber of Commerce. He is the vice president of the Florida Access Independent Physician Association and the president of the University of Miami's Alumni Association.

Moise works closely with the Haitian community and is involved in innumerable activities. He served on a chamber of commerce special task force to have Haitians removed from the Food and Drug Administration's AIDS risk list and is a member of the AIDS Haitian coalition. He is currently the chairman of the Haitian Affairs Committee of the Greater Miami Chamber of Commerce and is a founding member of the National Organization for the Advancement of Haitians (NOAH). Moise is also involved in humanitarian work in Haiti. He is the president and founder of Operation Kimbe Foundation, Inc., a nonprofit organization that provides medical support to Haitian-based organizations. For his philanthropic work and public service, Moise has received many accolades: the Entrepreneurial Excellence Award from the Jim Moran Institute for Global Entrepreneurship; the 1997 Black Business of the Year Award from the Greater Miami Chamber of Commerce; and the Pinnacle Award for Achievement and Professional Excellence.

Rodrigue Mortel (1933–), one of the leading specialists in women's cancer in the United States, was born in Haiti, where he received his medical degree from the Faculté de Médecine in 1960. After spending one year of graduate study in Montreal, Canada, he immigrated to the United States in 1963. From 1965 to 1968, he trained in the field of obstetrics and gynecology at the Hahnemann Medical College and Hospital in Philadelphia. From 1968 to 1970, he subspecialized in gynecologic oncology at the Memorial Sloan Kettering Cancer Center in New York City. He also had an opportunity to study in one of the best cancer laboratories at the University of Paris, where he was a fellow at the Ligue Nationale Française Contre le Cancer (French National League against Cancer).

In 1972, Mortel joined the Penn State University College of Medicine as an assistant professor, where he began an illustrious medical career, quickly earning the rank of full professor in the Department of Obstetrics and Gynecology in 1977. Six years later, he became the chair of that department, a position he occupied for nearly 13 years before being promoted to associate dean and director of the Penn State University Cancer Center in 1995. Mortel is one of the leading cancer surgeons in the United States, who has published 135 articles and book chapters. In 1988, he was one of the Robert Wood Johnson Health Policy Fellows selected by the Institute of Medicine of the National Academy of Sciences. He also served as a health aide to Congressman Sander Levin of the Health Subcommittee of the House Ways and Means Committee. In addition, since 1979 he has been a member of the advisory board of the National Cancer Institute. He occupies leadership positions in the most prestigious obstetrical and gynecological societies of the country; in 1994, he became the first foreign-born to be president of the American Society of Gynecologic Oncologists. In 1993 and 1997, he was named one of the Best 401 Doctors for Women in this country. For his innumerable achievements, Mortel has received many awards: the prestigious Horatio Alger Award, the Faculty Scholar Medal from Penn State University, the United States Public Health Service Award, the National Organization for the Advancement of Haitians (NOAH) Award for Excellence in Health and Education, the Sylvio Cator Award from the Haitian Canadian Foundation for Medical Education and Research, and the Doctor of the Decade Award from the South Florida Chapter of the Association of Physicians Abroad.

In spite of his renown, Mortel remains deeply rooted in his Haitian roots. He goes to Haiti quite often to volunteer his time and services. He is one of the two Haitians chosen to serve on the long-range planning committee for the Albert Schweitzer Hospital in Haiti. Mortel has recently created the Mortel Family Charitable Foundation, which is responsible for operating the Bons Samaritains (Good Samaritans), a school built in the city of St. Marc, Haiti, to serve the economically, socially, and educationally deprived children and adults of the region. Mortel traces his journey in a recently published book, *I Am from Haiti.*

Garry Pierre-Pierre (1962–   ), one of the most-respected Haitian American journalists and publisher of the *Haitian Times,* was born in Haiti. He came to the United States in 1973 and graduated from Elizabeth High School in New Jersey in 1981. He attended Florida Agricultural and Mechanical University where he obtained a bachelor of arts degree in history in 1989. He also gained additional experience as a Peace Corps volunteer in Togo, West Africa, where he lived from 1987 through 1989. Later, he had an opportunity to study Cuban politics and architecture in Havana, Cuba, through a program sponsored by Virginia Tech University in 1996. Additionally, he obtained certificates in marketing and marketing communications from the American Management Association in 1999.

A Pulitzer Prize–winning journalist, Pierre-Pierre has more than 15 years of experience as a reporter, including 6 years on the staff of the *New York Times*. Throughout his career, Pierre-Pierre has covered politics and national and international events. Pierre-Pierre first gained national visibility with his thorough coverage of Haiti during the early 1990s, as a reporter for the *Fort Lauderdale Sun-Sentinel*, where he worked from 1990 to late 1992. In January 1993, he joined the staff of the *New York Times*, where he focused on issues related to Haitian and Caribbean immigration in New York as well as those pertaining to crime and transportation. In addition, Pierre-Pierre covered stories such as the World Trade Center bombings, which won the paper a Pulitzer Prize for spot news. In 1997, Pierre-Pierre was one of the four *New York Times* reporters who covered the fall of Zaire's longtime dictator, Mobutu Sese Seko. In addition to his journalism experience, Pierre-Pierre has worked in the circulation department at the *New York Times* as direct marketing coordinator. He has lectured widely on Haiti and is often quoted by major news outlets, such as BBC and the *Los Angeles Times*. He is a member of the National Association of Black Journalists and of the Independent Press Association.

In 1999, Pierre-Pierre left the *New York Times* to start the *Haitian Times*, arguably the most important newspaper of the Haitian diaspora in the United States. The *Haitian Times* has been profiled in several newspapers and magazines around the country, including the *Miami Herald, Palm Beach Post, Newsday, New York Daily News,* and *Brill's Content.* For his outstanding contributions, Pierre-Pierre has received many accolades, including the *New York Times* Pulitzer Prize in 1994, the *New York Times* Publisher's Award in 1993 and 1995, and the First Place Award from the Associated Press for his coverage of Harlem fires in 1995.

Pierre-Richard Prosper (1963–   ), U.S. ambassador-at-large for war crimes, was born in Denver, Colorado, and later moved with his family to New York State. He graduated from Shenendehowa High School in Clifton Park, New York, in 1981. He attended Boston College, where he received a bachelor of arts degree in romance languages in 1985. Subsequently, he went on to earn a law degree from Pepperdine University School of Law in 1989.

Prosper began his law career in 1989 as a deputy district attorney for Los Angeles County. During his last two years in the District Attorney's Office (1992–1994), he prosecuted gang-related homicides for the Bureau of Special Operations, Hard Core Gang Division. Between 1994 and 1996, he was an assistant United States attorney for the Central District of California, where he was a prosecutor for the Drug Enforcement Task Force and investigated major international drug cartels. In 1996, Prosper joined the United Nations International Tribunal for Rwanda, as a prosecutor for war crimes. As lead prosecutor, he successfully prosecuted the first case of genocide under the 1948 Genocide Convention. Prosper is also credited for having convinced the tribunal to recognize rape committed in time of conflict as an act of genocide and a crime against humanity. Prosper gained a great deal of visibility and respect in the field of international law thanks to his outstanding work with the United Nations International Tribunal. Subsequently, he went to Washington to work for the U.S. Department of Justice, where he served as special assistant to the assistant attorney general for the criminal division. He also served as special council and policy advisor to the previous ambassador-at-large for war crimes issues. On May 16, 2001, Prosper was nominated by President Bush to be the next ambassador-at-large. Subsequently, he was confirmed by the Senate and was sworn in on July 13, 2001.

Prosper is the first Haitian American to have been hand picked by a U.S. president to serve as a member of his judicial team and to hold a high-ranking federal appointment. He is the frontline agent of U.S. justice around the world. In that capacity, he spends a great deal of his time away from his Washington, D.C., office and at the international tribunal in The Hague, the Netherlands, where the fate of Yugoslavian war criminal Slobodan Milosevic is being decided. Prosper has been recognized for his achievements and commitment to justice for all humanity by both his alma maters. In addition, he received a number of significant accolades from a variety of law associations and Haitian American organizations.

Yolly Roberson (1955–   ), a Florida state house representative, was born in Haiti. She came to the United States in 1976. Although she attended Dorchester High School in Boston for a brief period, she instead took the GED test and obtained a High School Equivalency Certificate. She then enrolled in a night program at Roxbury Community College to learn English and subsequently in a Laboratory Assistant Program at Northeastern University. In 1980, she went to Boston State College (which later merged with the University of Massachusetts–Boston) and earned a bachelor of science in nursing in 1983. She worked as a nurse for two years at Boston City Hospital until she decided to pursue a career in law, which led to her enrollment at New England Law School, where she received her law degree in 1988.

Roberson began her legal career as a public defender with the Committee for Public Counsel Services in Boston, where her main duties were to represent indigent clients accused of various felonies. In 1991, she moved to Miami to assist the staff of the Haitian Refugee Center in the fight for the rights of Haitian refugees. The following year, she joined the firm of Philipp J. Brutus, P.A, which later became the law firm of Brutus & Roberson. She also served as a senior assistant attorney general. Roberson currently owns and operates her law practice in North Miami, which focuses in the area of criminal defense, juvenile dependency and delinquency, family law, and real estate. She ran a successful campaign and was elected to the Florida State House of Representatives in 2002, thus becoming the second Haitian American in the Florida legislature and also the second Haitian American woman to win a seat in any state legislature.

Roberson's longtime commitment to public service is wel known throughout the Haitian community. She is a founding member of the Massachusetts Haitian American Nurses Association and the founder of the Haitian American Democratic Women's Club of Miami. She is a former president of the Haitian American Lawyers Association. She is involved in many prestigious organizations, including the Association of Trial Lawyers of America, the National Women's Political Caucus, the Florida Bar Association, the Academy of Florida Trial Lawyers, America's Association of Nurses, and the Women's Funds of Miami-Dade County, among others. She also serves as a board member of the Haitian American Foundation. Roberson has been appointed by Florida Governor Jeb Bush to serve on the National Governors Association Center for Best Practices Policy Academy that focuses on chronic diseases. In the State House of Representatives, she serves on the Joint Administrative Procedures committee, the Health Care committee, the Health Appropriations and Health Services subcommittees, and the Procedures committee and subcommittee on Ethics and Elections.

Fred Séraphin (1958–   ), a Miami-Dade County Circuit Court judge, was born in Haiti. He came to the United States in 1970 with his mother and siblings, fleeing the atrocities of the François "Papa Doc" Duvalier regime, which his family experienced firsthand. His father, a Duvalier political opponent, was murdered when Séraphin was only a year old; his older brother was imprisoned for nearly six years. Séraphin grew up in Jamaica, Queens, where he graduated from high school. He first attended Queens Borough Community College, where he received an associate degree, and later went to City College of the City University of New York to earn a bachelor of arts degree in 1983. Subsequently, he enrolled in law school at Hofstra University in Hempstead, New York, and earned his law degree in 1986.

Right after graduation, Séraphin joined the office of the Public Defender in Miami in August 1986, and worked in that office for 10 years as an assistant public defender. He was in private practice from 1991 to 1995, concentrating his efforts in the areas of criminal law, family law, and juvenile delinquency and dependency. During the same time, he was also an adjunct professor at Barry University in the Adult and Continuing Education Department. In 1995, he returned to Haiti for a few years to be part of the Department of Justice's team of prosecutors involved in the trials of several high-profile murder cases. On October 15, 2001, Florida Governor Jeb Bush appointed him to the County Court Judgeship for the Eleventh Judicial Circuit of Florida. He was sworn-in on November 20, 2001, becoming the first Haitian American judge in Miami-Dade County.

Séraphin belongs to several professional organizations, such as the Florida Bar Association, the Haitian Lawyers Association, the Cuban American Bar Association, and the Caribbean Bar Association. He is a sought-after speaker invited to lecture on the topic of human rights at many colleges and universities throughout the state of Florida. He remains active in the Haitian community as president of the Haitian Family Neighborhood Resource Center, and he is also involved with the Haitian Neighborhood Center. Additionally, he holds several positions within St. James Catholic Church. In 2001, he received the Haitian Lawyers Association Humanitarian Award.

Dumarsais (Dumas) Siméus (1939–   ), chairman and chief executive officer of Siméus Foods International, Inc. (SFI), the largest Black-owned food-processing company in the nation, was born in Haiti in a mud shack (as he wants people to know). He immigrated to the United States in 1961 to pursue a higher education. He obtained a bachelor of science degree in electrical engineering from Howard University in 1967 and a master's degree in business administration from the University of Chicago in 1972.

Siméus is one of a handful of Haitian-Americans who broke through the glass ceiling of corporate America. He held key management and executive positions in such companies as Atari, Inc., Rockwell International, Bendix Corporation, and others. He finished his corporate business career as president and chief operating officer of TLC Beatrice Foods, a $2.1 billion multinational corporation with operations in 25 countries. In 1996, Siméus followed his dream of becoming an entrepreneur, and he founded Siméus Food International, Inc., headquartered in Mansfield, Texas. SFI has over 700 employees and posts close to $200 million in sales.

In addition to devoting his energy to a successful business, Siméus is involved in a great many philanthropic activities both in the United States and in Haiti. For example, he established Minority Scholarship Funds at both the University of Chicago and Howard University, and his company regularly donates truckloads of food to food banks throughout the country. In 1999, he founded the Siméus Foundation, a nonprofit organization dedicated to providing medical care, food, clothing, and educational opportunities to the people of the Artibonite Valley in Haiti, where he was born. His foundation runs a full-time medical clinic in the region. Siméus serves as special advisor to congressional representatives and to the president of Haiti. For his humanitarian endeavors and successes, Siméus has received many prestigious awards, including the Ernst & Young Entrepreneur of the Year Award, the Distinguished Public Service Alumnus Award from the University of Chicago Graduate School of Business, the Haitian American Achievement Award from the National Organization for the Advancement of Haitians (NOAH), the National Coalition for Haitian Rights (NCHR) Exceptional Achievement Award, and an Award of Excellence from the Haitian American United for Progress Community Center (HAUP). He was also a finalist for the Horatio Alger Award.

Marie St. Fleur (1962–   ), a Massachusetts state house representative, was born in Haiti. She came to the United States in 1969 and graduated from Monsignor Ryan High School in Boston in 1980. She attended the University of Massachusetts at Amherst, where she earned a bachelor of arts in political science in 1984. Subsequently, she went to Boston College Law School, where she received her law degree in 1987.

After graduating from law school, St. Fleur worked as a law clerk for the Massachusetts Superior Court. She later served as an assistant district attorney in Middlesex County. In 1991, St. Fleur became an assistant attorney general in the Trial Division of the Office of the Attorney General. Subsequently, she became chief of the Unemployment Fraud Division, in charge of the investigation and prosecution of unemployment fraud. In 1999, St. Fleur was elected to the Massachusetts House of Representatives, becoming the first Haitian American ever to hold an elected seat in Massachusetts or a seat at any state legislature level. St. Fleur is well-known for her civic participation; she is a member of important boards, including the Democratic State Committee, the Women in Legislature Lobby (WiLL), the Women's Action for New Directions Committee, and the National Conference of State Legislators, where she serves on the Education Committee. She is also a member of the Speaker's Leadership Team in the Massachusetts House, and she chairs the Joint Committee on Education Arts and Humanities. St. Fleur is a former member of the Boston Bar Association Board of Trustees and Boston Bar Foundation, past president of the Massachusetts Black Lawyers Association, and a member of the Boston College Law School Black Alumni Association. She also served on the advisory board for a number of important projects and task forces: Project Hope, Action for Boston Community Development, and the YWCA of Boston. Additionally, she is a sought-after speaker invited by such institutions as the Massachusetts Bar Association, Boston College Law School, and the Kaplan Educational Center.

St. Fleur is one of the most visible members of the Haitian diaspora in the United States. She generously lends her support to Haitian organizations and is often seen at the forefront of Haitians' demonstrations for justice and equal treatment. She is a forceful speaker on a number of issues important to the community, such as education, economic development, and political empowerment. For her concern for social justice and many accomplishments, St. Fleur has received the Massachusetts School of Law Thurgood Marshall Leadership Award and has been featured as one of the Up & Coming Lawyers in the *Lawyers Weekly*. She has also been profiled in the International Institute's Dreams of Freedom Exhibit.

Rose-Marie Toussaint (1956–   ), a leading surgeon specializing in liver and kidney transplants, was born in Haiti. She came to the United States in 1971 and graduated from North Miami Beach Senior High School in 1974. She earned a bachelor of science degree in biology from Loyola University in New Orleans in 1978. Subsequently, she went to Howard University College of Medicine, where she obtained her medical degree (M.D.) in 1983. She also received training in the field of holistic medicine.

Toussaint, who is one of the two Black American women's liver transplant surgeons in the world, began her illustrious medical career in Washington, D.C., at Howard University, where she started as an assistant professor of surgery in 1991. She soon became associate director of the Howard University Hospital Transplant Center; in 1993 she was the lead surgeon of the first two combined liver/kidney transplants ever done in the nation's capital. Subsequently in 1997, she went into private practice, specializing in the care of liver transplant patients. She is credited for having maintained a patient survival rate higher than the national rate. In 2001, she left to take the position of general surgeon and medical director at the Norwegian American Hospital in Chicago and became affiliated with the Centre for Health Informatics and Multiprofessional Education (CHIME). Currently, Toussaint works as a bariatric surgeon (treatment of obesity) at the Forest Health/Bariatric Centers of Michigan in Canton.

Toussaint has contributed many articles on organ transplantation in professional journals. She is a member of prestigious medical societies such as the International Liver Transplantation Society, the National Kidney Foundation of the National Capital Area, the American Society of Transplant Surgeon, and the American College of Surgeons. She is also the founder and chairperson of the National Transplant Foundation and the medical director of HolisticDoctor, an organization that focuses on holistic health and healing. For her outstanding accomplishments, Toussaint has received many accolades: the Phenomenal Woman of the Year Award, the Global Initiative for Telemedicine's Medical Award of Merit, the Pioneers of Progress-Contributors in Transplantation, and the Outstanding Professional Achievement Award from the National Coalition for Haitian Rights (NCHR). She details her personal journey and her views on holistic, integrative, and alternative medicine in her book *Never Question the Miracle: A Surgeon's Story* (cowritten with Anthony E. Santaniello).

Marjorie Valbrun (1963–   ), a well-known immigration reporter for the *Wall Street Journal,* was born in Haiti. She came to the United States in 1969 and graduated from Spring Valley Senior High School in Spring Valley, New York, in 1981. She attended Long Island University/C.W. Post College, where she received a bachelor of arts degree in communications in 1985. Subsequently, she went to Columbia University Graduate School of Journalism, where she earned a master of science degree in journalism in 1986. In 1996, she was a Nieman Fellow at Harvard University, where she studied public policy and history.

Valbrun began her journalism career in 1987 as a municipal government reporter for the *Fort Lauderdale Sun-Sentinel.* In 1990, she joined the *Miami Herald,* where she covered the Haitian refugee crisis of the early 1990s. She also reported on Haiti's first free elections in December 1990 and the subsequent September 1991 military coup that sent President Aristide in exile in the United States. In addition, she covered higher education issues. In September 1992, Valbrun left the *Miami Herald* and took a position with the *Philadelphia Inquirer.* There, she covered a number of important issues, including welfare reform related to the state of Pennsylvania and the nation as a whole, poverty and unemployment matters in the city of Philadelphia, housing projects, and neighborhood crimes. She also reported on state government matters pertaining to health and social policy. In 1998, she relocated to Washington, D.C., and began her affiliation with the *Wall Street Journal* as an immigration reporter. Lately, Valbrun has been covering the economic, social, and political impact of immigration since September 11, 2001. She focuses on immigration laws and how they affect foreign students, business individuals, tourists, and thousands of refugees fleeing war-torn countries.

In 2001, Valbrun was awarded an Alicia Patterson Research Fellowship for journalists. Consequently, she researched the emergence of Haitian Americans into the American political system and their political coming of age in the United States; she wrote a number of stories on the topic. She is a member of the National Organization of Black Journalists. For her significant achievements in the field of journalism, Valbrun has received a number of prestigious awards, including the 1992 First Place Award for international reporting on Haiti from the National Association of Black Journalists and the 1994 Journalist of the Year Award from the Garden State Association of Black Journalists. She serves as a mentor to young journalists and Haitian American students who want to be journalists.

Michaelle Vincent (1952–   ), a district instructional supervisor in the Division of Bilingual Education and World Languages of the Miami-Dade County Public Schools, was born in Haiti. She came to the United States in 1965 and graduated from George W. Wingate High School in Brooklyn, New York, in 1970. She attended York College of the City University of New York, where she obtained a bachelor of arts degree in French and education in 1974. After working for many years as an educator, she went back to school and earned a master of science degree in TESOL (Teaching English to Speakers of Other Languages) from the University of Miami in 1992.

Vincent began her teaching career in 1975 as a bilingual teacher at South Shore High School in Brooklyn. In 1979, she moved to Miami and joined the Miami-Dade County Public Schools, where she taught reading and writing until 1983. During the following two years, she occupied the position of head teacher for English as a Second Language (ESL) in the Cuban and Haitian Entrant Programs at Florida International University. In 1983, she joined the City of Miami Police Department as a community involvement specialist in charge of developing informational seminars for Haitians on traffic rules and laws, child abuse, spousal abuse, and parenting skills. In 1986, she went back to the Miami-Dade County Public Schools as an intergroup relations specialist, where she was the liaison between teachers and administrators. Vincent gained a great deal of respect and visibility in the Haitian community for her work as a parent outreach coordinator and as host of a popular radio program, *Radyo Lekòl* (School Radio), that disseminated various information related to school issues to Haitian parents throughout the

Miami-Dade County area. In 1992, Vincent became a bilingual instructional supervisor, in charge of the development of Haitian Creole materials used in language arts programs at the elementary level; in 1996, she was promoted to district supervisor. One of her major tasks is staff development, and she is also involved in Haitian Creole bilingual teacher training. Vincent is credited for having played a significant role in the promotion of bilingual education programs for Haitian students enrolled in the Miami-Dade County public school system.

Vincent is well-known to Haitian teachers in the Miami area and belongs to various organizations, such as the Commission on the Status of Women, and the Association of Haitian Educators of Dade County. She is also involved in educational centers in Haiti. For her outstanding contributions, she has received several awards—for example, a 1998 Proclamation from the Miami-Dade County Commissioner for her work as an administrator in the school system, a 1996 Excellence in Education Award from Oganization Ayisyen Tèt Ansanm Nan Miyami (Organization of Haitians Together in Miami), and a Trophy of Merit for her work with *Radyo Lekòl.*

Works Cited

Alba, Richard D. 1990. *Ethnic Identity: The Transformation of White America.* New Haven, CT: Yale University Press.

Alexis, Gérald. 2000. *Peintres Haïtiens* (English version). Paris: Éditions Cercle d'Art.

Arthur, Charles. 2002. *Haiti in Focus: A Guide to the People, Politics, and Culture.* New York: Interlink Books.

Arthur, Charles, and J. Michael Dash. 1999. *Libète: A Haiti Anthology.* Princeton, NJ: Markus Wiener.

Averill, Gage. 1997. *A Day for the Hunter, A Day for the Prey: Popular Music and Power in Haiti.* Chicago: University of Chicago Press.

Basch, Linda, Nina Glick Schiller, and Cristina Szanton Blanc. 1994. *Nations Unbound: Transnational Projects, Postcolonial Predicaments, and Deterritorialized Nations-States.* Langhorne, PA: Gordon and Breach.

Boston Redevelopment Authority. 1999. *Gateway City: Boston Immigrants 1988–1998.* Boston: Department of Redevelopment Authority.

Brown, Karen McCarthy. 2001. *Mama Lola: A Vodou Priestess in Brooklyn,* 2nd ed. Berkeley: University of California Press.

Brownstone, David. M., and Irene M. Franck. 2001. *Facts about American Immigration.* New York: H. W. Wilson.

Charles, Carole. 1990. "A Transnational Dialectic of Race, Class, and Ethnicity: Patterns of Identity and Forms of Consciousness among Haitian Migrants in New York City." Ph.D. Diss., State University of New York at Binghamton.

Cosentino, Donald. 1995. *Sacred Arts of Haitian Vodou.* Los Angeles: UCLA Fowler Museum.

Dash, J. Michael. 2001. *Culture and Customs of Haiti.* Westport, CT: Greenwood.

Desmangles, Leslie. 1992. *The Faces of the Gods.* Chapel Hill: University of North Carolina Press.

Dupuy, Alex. 1989. *Haiti in the World Economy: Class, Race, and Underdevelopment since 1700.* Boulder, CO: Westview.

Edmonston, Barry, and Jeffrey S. Passel. 1994. *Immigration and Ethnicity. The Integration of America's Newest Arrivals.* Washington, D.C.: Urban Institute Press.

Farmer, Paul. 1992. *AIDS and Accusation: Haiti and the Geography of Blame.* Berkeley: University of California Press.

Fatton, Robert Jr. 2002. *Haiti's Predatory Republic: The Unending Transition to Democracy.* Boulder, CO: Lynne Rienner.

Ferguson, James. 1987. *Papa Doc, Baby Doc: Haiti and the Duvaliers.* New York: Basil Blackwell.

Fick, Carolyn. 1990. *The Making of Haiti: The Saint-Domingue Revolution from Below.* Knoxville: University of Tennessee Press.

Fleurant, Gerdès. 1996. *Dancing Spirits: Rhythms and Rituals of Haitian Vodun, the Rada Rite.* Westport, CT: Greenwood.

Galembo, Phyllis. 1998. *Vodou: Visions and Voices of Haiti.* Berkeley: Ten Speed.

Geggus, David Patrick. 2002. *Haitian Revolutionary Studies.* Bloomington: Indiana University Press.

Heinl, Robert Debs, Nancy Gordon Heinl, and Michael Heinl. 1995. *Written in Blood: The Story of the Haitian People 1492–1995,* 2nd ed. Lanham, MD: University Press of America.

Hunt, Alfred. 1988. *Haiti's Influence on Antebellum America: Slumbering Volcano in the Caribbean.* Baton Rouge: Louisiana State University Press.

James, Cyril Lionel Robert. 1980. *The Black Jacobins: Toussaint L'Ouverture and the San Domingo Revolution,* 3rd ed. London: Allison and Busby.

Laguerre, Michel S. 1984. *American Odyssey: Haitians in New York City.* Ithaca, NY: Cornell University Press.

LeMay, Michael, and Elliott Robert Barkan. 1999. *U.S. Immigration and Naturalization Laws and Issues: A Documented History.* Westport, CT: Greenwood.

Massachussetts Office of Refugee and Immigrant Health, Bureau of Family and Community Health, and Massachussetts Department of Public Health. 1998. *Refugees and Immigrants in Massachussetts: An Overview of Selected Communities.* Boston, MA: Office of Refugee and Immigrant Health.

McAlister, Elizabeth. 2002. *Rara: Vodou, Power, and Performance in Haiti and Its Diaspora.* Berkely: University of California Press.

Miller, Jake C. 1984. *The Plight of Haitian Refugees.* New York: Praeger.

Moreau de Saint-Méry, Médéric-Louis-Élie. 1958. [1797–1798]. *Description de la partie française de l'île de Saint-Domingue.* Vols. 1–2. Paris: Société de l'histoire des colonies françaises.

Nachman, Steven R. 1997. Review of Zéphir's *Haitian Immigrants in Black America: A Sociological and Sociolinguistic Portrait. Journal of Anthropological Research* 53, 1: 116–19.

Nahirny, Vladimir C., and Joshua A. Fishman. 1996. (Reprint of 1965). "American Immigrant Groups: Ethnic Identification and the Problems of Generations." In *Theories of Ethnicity: A Classical Reader,* edited by Werner Sollors, 266–81. New York: New York University Press.

New York City Department of City Planning. 1992. *The Newest New Yorkers: An Analysis of Immigration into New York City during the 1980s.* New York: Department of City Planning.

Nicholls, David. 1996. *From Dessalines to Duvalier: Race, Colour and National Independence in Haiti,* rev. ed. New Brunswick, NJ: Rutgers University Press.

Pamphile, Leon D. 2001. *Haitians and African Americans: A Heritage of Tragedy and Hope.* Gainesville: University Press of Florida.

Plummer, Brenda Gayle. 1992. *Haiti and the United States: The Psychological Moment.* Athens: University of Georgia Press.

Quaife, M. Milo. 1933. *Checagou: From Indian Wigwam to Modern City. 1673–1835.* Chicago: University of Chicago Press.

Reid, Ira De A. 1939. *The Negroe Immigrant: His Background, Characteristics, and Social Adjustments, 1899–1937.* New York: Columbia University Press.

Rogozinski, Jan. 1999. *A Brief History of the Caribbean: From the Arawak and the Carib to the Present.* New York: Facts on File.

Stepick, Alex. 1986. *Haitian Refugees in the U.S.* Report No. 52. London: Minority Rights Group.

Stepick, Alex, Guillermo Grenier, Max Castro, and Marvin Dunn. 2003. *This Land Is Our Land: Immigrants and Power in Miami.* Berkeley: University of California Press.

Takaki, Ronald. 1993. *A Different Mirror: A History of Multicultural America.* Boston: Little, Brown.

———. 1998. *A Larger Memory: A History of Our Diversity with Voices.* Boston: Little, Brown.

Torres-Saillant, Silvio, and Ramona Hernández. 1998. *The Dominican Americans.* Wesport, CT: Greenwood.

Trouillot, Michel-Rolph. 1990. *Haiti: State against Nation.* New York: Monthly Review.

United States Department of Justice. Immigration and Naturalization Service. 1960–2000. *Statistical Yearbook.* Washington, D.C.: Government Printing Office.

Walker, Juliet E. K. 1999. "African Americans." In *A Nation of Peoples: A Sourcebook on America's Multicultural Heritage,* edited by Elliott Robert Barkan, 19–47. Westport, CT: Greenwood.

Waters, Mary C. 1996. "Ethnic and Racial Identities of Second-Generation Black Immigrants in New York City." In *The New Second Generation,* edited by Alejandro Portes, 171–96. New York: Russell Sage Foundation.

Weistein, Brian, and Aaron Segal. 1984. *Haiti: Political Failures, Cultural Successes.* New York: Praeger.

———. 1992. *Haiti: The Failure of Politics.* New York: Praeger.

Zéphir, Flore. 1996. *Haitian Immigrants in Black America: A Sociolinguistic and Sociological Portrait.* Westport, CT: Bergin and Garvey.

———. 1997. "The Social Value of French for Biligual Haitian Immigrants." *The French Review* 70, 3: 395–406.

———. 2001. *Trends in Ethnic Identification among Second-Generation Haitian Immigrants in New York City.* Westport, CT: Bergin and Garvey.

Index

About the Author

FLORE ZÉPHIR is Professor of Romance Languages and African Diaspora Studies at the University of Missouri, Columbia.

Other Titles in
The New Americans Series
Ronald H. Bayor, Series Editor

The Cuban Americans
Miguel Gonzalez-Pando

The Dominican Americans
Silvio Torres-Saillant and Ramona Hernández

The Taiwanese Americans
Franklin Ng

The Korean Americans
Won Moo Hurh

The Soviet Jewish Americans
Annelise Orleck

The Vietnamese Americans
Hien Duc Do

The Filipino Americans
Barbara M. Posadas

The Chinese Americans
Benson Tong

Puerto Ricans in the United States
Maria E. Perez y Gonzalez

The West Indian Americans
Holger Henke

The Mexican Americans
Alma M. Garcia

The Nigerian Americans
Kalu Ogbaa